AF480489

Endorsements

All I can say is, "Wow!"

The Easter Story: The Son is unlike any book I've ever read. Biblically sound and wonderfully written, it speaks to readers at every stage of faith, offering practical and meaningful insights on each page. Gabe has a masterful way of getting to the heart of each story and then clearly explaining why it matters to us today. Each chapter points readers back to Scripture with clear chapter and verse, inviting them to engage God's Word for themselves.

In a world where many still believe Easter is about rabbits and chocolate-filled plastic eggs, this book gently but clearly reminds us of what Easter truly is and why this story needs to be told in a clear, meaningful, and biblically sound way.

Peter Knutson CFP, CLTC, AIF
Partner Advisor
Allworth Financial

As someone who once wrestled with where to begin reading the Bible, I am grateful for the clear and approachable way *The Easter Story: The Son* is written. Across forty-seven days of readings, Gabe carefully and faithfully guides readers through the life, death, resurrection, and ascension of Jesus. Each reading helps anchor the heart in the truth of who Jesus is and why these moments matter so deeply.

My favorite element of this devotional is the "Prayer to End" in each reading, which invites readers to slow down, reflect, and respond to God's Word. This book is a wonderful resource for families, creating space for intentional faith conversations and helping parents walk alongside their children as they grow in their understanding of the gospel. *The Easter Story: The Son* is a valuable tool for teaching the next generation the story of our Savior and for guiding families as they engage deeply with the gospel together.

Christian Rhoades
High School Director
Leawood Presbyterian Church

Gabe Rodriguez has crafted a remarkable gift for a new generation of Bible readers in *The Easter Story: The Son*. Through forty-seven easy-to-read chapters, Gabe breathes fresh life into Jesus' journey, from His childhood teachings in the temple to His glorious ascension. Each moment is made accessible and meaningful for young readers while also creating a reflective, contemplative space for mature readers to encounter these timeless truths anew.

The book's thoughtful structure, combining clear biblical storytelling, "Why This Story Matters" reflections, and guided prayers, creates a natural bridge for the next generation as they discover how these sacred stories connect and unfold. This is more than a retelling of Scripture; it is an invitation to encounter the heart of the Easter story in a way that feels both personal and lasting.

Isaac Miranda
TRO Marketing Agency
Founder and CEO

Having studied Scripture with Gabe over the past several years, I've seen firsthand his unique ability to interpret the Bible in ways that are both easy to understand and meaningful for our modern, everyday lives. In his latest book, *The Easter Story: The Son*, Gabe walks readers through the life of Jesus and the stories of the New Testament in a way that draws us closer to understanding who Jesus is, why God sent Him, and how His life and teachings continue to shape and guide us today. Throughout the journey, Gabe consistently points us back to the central truth of the gospel: that Jesus came to restore our relationship with God, and that through Christ, God is with us and for us.

The "Why This Story Matters" sections are especially impactful. These reflections help both youth and adults see how the stories of Jesus connect directly to their lives today. They gently remind us that God is present with us through both the highs and the lows that life brings our way.

Lucas Gillen
Partner
TREKK Design Group

THE EASTER STORY

The Son

Gabe Rodriguez

The Easter Story
The Son
Gabe Rodriguez

3 in 1 Press, Shawnee, Kansas
Copyright ©2026 Gabe Rodriguez
All rights reserved.

Scripture quotations taken from The Holy Bible, New International Version®, NIV®. Copyright © 1973, 1978, 1984, 2011 by Biblica, Inc. Used with permission of Zondervan. All rights reserved worldwide. www.zondervan.com

Editor: Kim Fletcher

Cover and Interior design: DavisCreativePublishing.com

Names: Rodriguez, Gabe, author.

Publisher's Cataloging-in-Publication
Title: The Easter story. The Son / Gabe Rodriguez.

Other titles: Son

Description: Shawnee, Kansas : 3 in 1 Press, [2026] | Includes bibliographical references.

Identifiers: LCCN: 2026902081 | ISBN: 9798993520230 (paperback) | 9798993520254 (hardback) | 9798993520247 (ebook)

Subjects: LCSH: Jesus Christ--Teachings. | Jesus Christ--Resurrection--Biblical teaching. | Easter. | God (Christianity) | LCGFT: Devotional literature. | BISAC: RELIGION / Holidays / Easter & Lent. | RELIGION / Christian Living / Devotional. | RELIGION / Christian Education / General.

Classification: LCC: BS2415 .R64 2026 | DDC: 232.954--dc23

DEDICATION

To Benjamin and Samuel,
my inspiration for writing the Trinity series.
Being your dad is the greatest
blessing of my life.

Table of Contents

Foreword

The Easter story is not merely a moment in history — it is the defining story of humanity. It is the story of love poured out, hope secured, and redemption accomplished through the life, death, resurrection, and ascension of Jesus Christ. Yet, for a story so central to our faith, it can sometimes feel distant from our everyday lives, especially within the rhythms of family life. *The Easter Story: The Son* bridges that gap in a beautiful, intentional, and deeply relational way.

This book begins where Scripture first gives us a glimpse into the heart of Jesus as a young boy — twelve years old, found in the temple, fully engaged in His Father's business. From that sacred moment of obedience and identity, Gabe Rodriguez leads readers through a chronological journey of Christ's life, ministry, sacrifice, and ultimate victory. Page by page, families are invited to walk with Jesus from the temple courts to the cross, from the empty tomb to His glorious ascension into heaven.

What makes *The Easter Story: The Son* so powerful is not only what it tells us, but how it is told. The timeline format allows readers — children and adults alike — to see the intentional unfolding of God's redemptive plan. It slows the story down, creating space to reflect, ask questions, and truly grasp the weight and wonder of who Jesus is and why He came. This is not a rushed retelling; it is an invitation to dwell in the story together.

I read this book not only as a pastor, but as a pastor's kid now raising pastor's kids of my own. I understand firsthand the deep responsibility — and sacred opportunity — of discipling our children while navigating the demands of ministry. There is a unique tension in leading others spiritually while ensuring that faith is being cultivated authentically within the walls of our own homes. Tools like this matter deeply because they help bridge that gap, giving parents language, structure, and confidence to disciple their children as God leads.

Designed to be read as a family, *The Easter Story: The Son* becomes more than a devotional — it becomes a shared faith experience. The family scroll included in the back of the book is a sacred and meaningful addition, reminding us that faith is meant to be remembered, recorded, and passed down. It creates a tangible way for families to document how the Easter story has impacted their lives and to preserve those moments for future generations. Long after the book is closed, the story of Jesus continues to live on through the words written there.

This book is the second installment in the Trinity series — *The Christmas Story: The Father*, *The Easter Story: The Son*, and *The Thanksgiving Story: The Holy Spirit*. The trilogy was born from a father's desire to connect more deeply with God and with his sons through a relationship with Christ. Gabe Rodriguez writes not just as an author but as a father who understands that the greatest legacy we can leave our children is a faith that is lived, shared, and deeply rooted in Jesus.

The Easter Story: The Son is an incredible tool for fathers, mothers, and children. It empowers parents to disciple their children with clarity and intentionality, while inviting children into the greatest story ever told — not as distant observers, but as participants in God's redemptive work.

My prayer is that this book would be read aloud around tables, revisited year after year, and treasured as a family heirloom. May it draw hearts closer to Jesus and to one another. And may the story of Christ — from a faithful boy in the temple to the risen King who ascended into heaven — remain alive in families for generations to come.

Robin Allen
Associate Pastor
City Center Church – Lenexa, Kansas

Preface

My journey into writing did not start with a desire to become an author. It started with God waking up something inside me. After decades of what I would call a "lukewarm" faith, God surrounded me with the right people at the right time, faithful men who challenged me, a church that felt like family, and a growing desire to truly follow Jesus. My faith began to come alive in a way I had not experienced before.

As my relationship with God deepened, I began to notice something important in my own home. I started to see parts of my younger self reflected in my boys. Growing up, my faith was encouraged, but I had to piece together much of my spiritual understanding on my own. That realization made me pause and reflect on how faith was being formed in our family.

While my wife has faithfully poured into our boys, I recognized that without greater intention and guidance, it would be easy for them to grow up knowing about God without fully understanding who He is or how deeply He loves them. I did not want faith to feel distant, confusing, or disconnected from everyday life. I wanted our children to experience a faith that was lived, shared, and nurtured together, not something they felt they had to navigate alone.

As my faith grew, I also found myself more open and willing to talk about it with others, with siblings, in-laws, friends, and extended family. Those conversations were honest and meaningful. We shared our different church experiences, wrestled with Scripture, reflected on how we were raised, and talked about what we wish we had understood sooner. It was through these thoughtful discussions, sometimes marked by agreement and sometimes by differences, that my faith continued to deepen. Those moments, as much as anything else, helped shape my desire to write these stories and share them with others.

When I first sat down to write, my only goal was to help my boys understand the true meaning of Christmas in a way they could follow, enjoy, and remember. That became the first book in this series, *The Christmas Story: The Father*.

But God was just getting started.

The Holy Spirit continued stirring something inside me. My faith was growing, and God helped me see that Christmas is only the beginning. The life of Jesus, His teachings, miracles, sacrifice on the cross, resurrection, and sending of the Holy Spirit, is the greatest story ever told. It is the story of the Trinity: the Father who loves us, the Son who saves us, and the Spirit who guides and strengthens us.

Jesus often spoke in parables so people could understand truth in a simple and memorable way. He knew that stories have a way of settling into the heart and staying with us long after the moment has passed. He taught about hearing God's Word but losing it when life becomes difficult, about receiving it with excitement only to walk away later, and about the danger of seeing truth clearly and still forgetting it once we turn away.

I did not want that for my children, or for anyone's children. I did not want families to hear the words of Jesus without truly understanding His purpose for their lives, or to forget His voice when life becomes busy, stressful, or uncertain. That is why this book was written, so the truths Jesus taught can be understood, remembered, and carried forward; not just read once, but held onto for a lifetime.

The Easter Story: The Son is meant to help kids, families, and anyone seeking to better understand Jesus' ministry in a way that is engaging, simple, and true to Scripture. It is also written for parents and caregivers who want to lead their families faithfully, even if they feel they are still learning and growing themselves. You do not need to have all the answers to begin. If you are seeking, learning, and willing to walk alongside those in your care, this story is for you, too.

At times, I questioned whether I was the right person for this. I do not have everything figured out spiritually. I am still growing. But God kept reminding me of Jesus' promise that when we go out and share His truth, "the Holy Spirit will teach you at that time what you should say" (Luke 12:12). I felt led not to wait another year, not to wait until I felt more prepared, but to be faithful to the calling God placed on my heart in this season.

So whether you are a parent reading aloud, a child listening with curiosity, or someone returning to faith after years of searching, my hope is that these pages help you draw closer to Jesus. I pray that the story of His life and His love becomes part of your rhythm and tradition, not just at Easter, but every day of your life.

How To Use This Book

Overview

First and foremost, this book is not meant to replace the Bible, the living Word of God. The Bible holds immeasurable value. Its pages are filled with life lessons, truth, and history that serve as our moral compass, showing us how to live the lives God intends for us.

The Easter Story: The Son is designed as an overview of Jesus' ministry. It presents key stories in a clear, chronological, and easily digestible format, connecting one story to the next so readers can better understand the timeline and the life Jesus was called to live. Included are some of the most well-known biblical events from His life, including parables, teachings, healings, miracles, and His betrayal, all of which come together as part of God's larger plan, ultimately leading to our salvation and eternal life with the Father.

The purpose of this book is to help reveal the "why" behind Jesus' ministry, why He had to die on the cross for our sins, and to help us remember the true meaning of Easter. Humanity, in all its brokenness, could never save or reconcile itself to the Father. So God sent His Son, Jesus Christ, a perfect and blameless sacrifice, to become the Savior of the world.

My hope is that everyone who reads this book will:

- Understand who God is
- See how loving God truly is
- Remember why Jesus came
- Learn from the way Jesus lived His life, and apply His example to our own lives
- Realize that God sees each of us and that we all matter
- Understand that each of us was created with a purpose
- Use this book as a guide to the New Testament
- See the Bible not as an ancient book of the past, but as a living guide for today
- Create meaningful Christian family traditions

When Should I Read This Book?

Every Easter Season

This book is designed to be read each year in the weeks leading up to Easter. It invites individuals and families to slow down, reflect, and return to the true meaning of Easter, creating a meaningful tradition that keeps Jesus' life and ministry at the center of the season. Families and readers are encouraged to move at a pace that fits their season of life, allowing time for conversation, reflection, and rest along the way.

Any Time of Year

Although written with the Easter season in mind, this book can be read at any time of the year to gain a deeper understanding of Jesus' ministry, life, and work through His disciples.

For Bible Study

The Easter Story: The Son can also be used as a forty-seven-day Bible study. Read and then gather to reflect on what stood out. Use the "Why This Story Matters" and "Pause & Reflect" sections to guide conversations and personal reflection. Ask questions such as: How does this story apply to my life or my family? What part of the story speaks most clearly to my heart? The Bible references included with each reading also invite you to explore Scripture more deeply on your own. Use these moments to grow together in faith with family and friends.

Pause & Reflect

The five Pause & Reflect sections are intentionally placed throughout the book to reinforce key themes from Jesus' ministry. These moments create space to slow down, absorb His words and actions, and thoughtfully connect them to everyday life. Rather than immediately moving on to the next story, the Pause & Reflect readings invite readers to internalize what they have been learning and consider how it applies personally.

Throughout Scripture, Jesus often followed this same rhythm. He taught, then withdrew. He spoke truth, then invited reflection. Each Pause & Reflect section gives readers the opportunity to mirror that pattern in their own lives. This order is not accidental. It is the very way Jesus walked with His disciples, patiently leading them step by step toward a deeper and more faithful life.

1. Invitation

Jesus came for everyone. This establishes access. No barriers. No qualifications.

2. Surrender

Bring Him our burdens and find true rest. Once access is established, the natural response is surrender.

3. Discipleship

Know His truth and follow His ways. Relationship with Jesus leads to obedience, not the other way around.

4. Transformation

Transformed hearts learn to hear God's calling. This reflects sanctification, the lifelong process of being shaped and changed by God as we grow to listen for His voice and live more like Christ.

5. Mission

A bold voice empowered by the Spirit. This points forward toward mission and Pentecost without jumping ahead of the story.

What Is the Purpose of the Family Scroll?

Many of us have family traditions passed down through generations — recipes shared, heirlooms treasured, or stories retold. These keepsakes remind us of where we come from and the people who came before us. But how do we pass on our faith to the next generation?

As a parent, I have worked hard to teach my boys courtesy and good manners, opening the door for others, saying "please" and "thank you," offering a firm handshake, and keeping their elbows off the table. Yet I have often wondered, how do I ensure they also inherit my faith? How will they one day pass that faith on to their own families?

Those questions inspired what I call the Family Scroll at the end of this book. It is a space for you and your family to record your belief in the Trinity series I have been led to write: the Father, the Son, and the Holy Spirit. Like a family tree, it allows you to document who you believe in, where you came from, what your purpose is, and why Jesus was sent for you.

My hope is that as you read *The Easter Story: The Son*, you will record the year you first read and believed each story, then continue marking each time you revisit them, whether annually or multiple times throughout the year. Over time, your Family Scroll will tell a beautiful story of faith handed down generation after generation, so that one day your children, grandchildren, and great-grandchildren will see their names among those who believed before them.

Imagine being a young boy or girl reading *The Easter Story: The Son* for the first time, and at the end of the book, signing your name beneath those of family members who have read and believed these same stories for decades, or even centuries. That is powerful. That is legacy. That is faith passed on.

What Do the Colors on the Cover Mean?

Blue (The Father)

Blue is the color of Advent, the season of hope, peace, joy, and love leading up to Christmas. It symbolizes the hope we have in the Father, whose promise was fulfilled through the birth of His Son, Jesus Christ.

Green (The Son)

The color green symbolizes new life and renewal, seen each spring as the earth comes alive after winter. For believers, it represents spiritual growth, revival, and a faith that continues to mature throughout life. Through our belief in Jesus Christ, we are made new and grow daily in His grace.

Red (The Holy Spirit)

Red symbolizes both power and sacrifice. It represents the fire of the Holy Spirit that came down at Pentecost and the courage it gave the apostles to spread the Gospel. Red also reminds us of the blood of Jesus poured out for our sins and the sacrifice of those who carried, and continue to carry, His message to the ends of the earth.

Why Are There Dates at the Beginning of Each Story?

Dates found throughout this book are approximate. Biblical scholars and historians often differ on the exact years of events in Scripture. I do not claim to be a historian, and the dates provided are not meant to be exact. They are directionally accurate and organized chronologically to help readers follow the timeline of God's unfolding story.

You will see the symbol (~) before each date, acknowledging that while specific years may vary slightly depending on the source, the heart and message of each story remain unchanged.

Definitions

Grace is receiving something we do not deserve. It is God giving us favor, forgiveness, and new life, not because of what we have done, but because of who He is. Grace cannot be earned; it is freely given.

Example of Grace

Jesus' death on the cross is the greatest example of grace. We did not deserve forgiveness, yet Jesus took our place so we could be restored into a relationship with God.

Mercy is not receiving the punishment we deserve. Biblically, it is God withholding judgment, choosing compassion over condemnation, even when justice or the law would allow punishment.

Example of Mercy

By accepting Matthew the tax collector's invitation to dinner, Jesus showed mercy by willingly sitting with an outcast and inviting him into a relationship instead of rejecting him.

Introduction: The Son

In *The Christmas Story: The Father*, the first book in the Trinity series, we learned how sin entered the world through Adam and Eve and how it separated us from God. We saw how people tried to follow God's ways for generations but continued to struggle. Even those who were chosen to lead God's people drifted from Him, placing rules and religion above love and relationship.

But none of this surprised God.

Long before Jesus was born, God promised a Savior, One who would make things right again. Through the prophets, God said the Messiah would be born in Bethlehem, come from the line of King David, be rejected by His own people, suffer greatly, and ultimately give His life for our sins. Every part of Jesus' life and mission was written in Scripture hundreds of years before He arrived.

Jesus did not come into the world simply to be a good teacher or a wise leader. He came with a mission to save us, restore us, and bring us back into a close and loving relationship with God. His story is the heartbeat of the Bible, the center of God's plan from the very beginning.

When Jesus finally came, many people, including the religious leaders, could not see the truth standing right in front of them. They read the Scriptures but missed the Savior they longed for. Their hearts were focused on earthly desires like position, authority, and applause from others. Faith became something performed, instead of believed.

Those who looked for the Messiah believed He would be a powerful king or a fearless warrior who would destroy Israel's enemies and restore its earthly glory. They assumed He would come only for the Jewish people, not for the Gentiles or the broken, forgotten, and hurting. They imagined a Savior who would conquer Rome, punish those who had oppressed them, and restore the throne of David through military might.

But Jesus came in a completely different way. He came not to be served but to serve. He came as a humble carpenter from Nazareth, not a famous ruler from Jerusalem. He cared for the forgotten, noticed the lonely, healed the sick, welcomed sinners, and lifted up the poor, the orphan, and the widow. Instead of overthrowing nations, He came to overthrow sin. Instead of building a kingdom on earth, He came to open the way to the Kingdom of God.

Because many held on to their own idea of who the Messiah should be, they did not recognize Jesus when He came. He faced rejection, accusation, betrayal, and suffering. Yet, He stayed faithful to the mission the Father had given Him.

Every moment of His ministry pointed people back to God.

When the time came, Jesus gave His life on the cross so we could be forgiven, rescued from sin, and welcomed into a relationship with God forever. But death could not hold Him. He rose again, conquering darkness, so we could one day live with Him for eternity.

The Easter Story: The Son tells that life-changing story.

In the Year of Our Lord, ~AD 12

Jesus in the Temple — My Father's House

Joseph and His Family Return to Israel

Toward the end of King Herod's reign, Joseph and his family sought safety in Egypt to avoid King Herod's evil decrees (Matthew 2). After thirty-seven years of ruling ruthlessly over the people of Israel, King Herod finally died. Soon after his death, an angel appeared to Joseph in a dream, telling him, "Get up, take the child and his mother and go to the land of Israel, for those who were trying to take the child's life are dead" (Matthew 2:19–20).

Now that it was safe to return, Joseph packed up his family and set out for the long, strenuous journey back to Israel. But instead of heading back to Joseph's hometown of Bethlehem, he decided to settle his family in the small town of Nazareth in Galilee (Matthew 2:22–23). There, Jesus was raised, not in a castle or among the rich, but in a humble, loving home where He learned carpentry and obedience to His parents and God (Luke 2:51).

Growing in the Lord's Favor

Jesus grew up and was educated by His parents, like other children in His community. In those days, Jewish boys began memorizing Scripture at a very young age. By the time they were five or six years old, they were required to memorize the first five books of the Bible, which are called the Torah. Memorizing entire passages was a normal part of a young Jewish boy's life, and only the most talented boys were selected to train under a rabbi (teacher), a senior religious leader.

Today, most boys dream of becoming an astronaut or a professional athlete when they grow up. But in Jesus' time, most boys wanted to be a respected religious leader, a role that required many years of study and discipline. The boys who were selected spent the rest of their lives instructing and training others in the synagogue, interpreting the teachings of Moses, and ensuring people followed the current religious laws.

People in the community could tell there was something different about Jesus. Even as a boy, His heart burned with a love for God that far surpassed other boys His age (Luke 2:40).

The Big Surprise After the Passover Festival

When Jesus was twelve years old, His extended family traveled to Jerusalem to take part in the Passover festival (Luke 2:41–42). The Passover was a special time for Jewish families to come together and remember how God had delivered His people from slavery in Egypt (Exodus 12:40–42).

Once the festival was over, Mary and Joseph's extended family began the long journey back to Nazareth. Jesus' parents assumed He was among them, but after a full day of traveling, they soon realized He wasn't. Worry quickly set in.

The next day, Mary and Joseph returned to Jerusalem in hopes of finding their Son. After searching for Him for three days, they found Jesus in the Temple, not lost or afraid, but sitting as a student among the teachers, absorbing everything they taught (Luke 2:46). Jesus listened carefully, and if He heard something He didn't agree with or understand, He confidently asked questions and gave His interpretations of the Scriptures. All the teachers and those in attendance were amazed at His understanding, questions, and the way He spoke (Luke 2:47).

When Mary approached Jesus, she was frustrated with Him and asked why He had stayed behind without letting them know. Jesus answered gently, "Didn't you know I had to be in my Father's house?" (Luke 2:49). Mary and Joseph were confused by His response and didn't know what He meant. But Jesus wasn't confused. Even at such a young age, He already knew who He was and that God was His real father.

Still, Jesus wanted to respect and obey His parents. He left the Temple and returned home with them. Once back in Nazareth, He continued to grow in wisdom, in stature, and in God's favor, as He prepared for all that was to come (Luke 2:51–52).

Why This Story Matters

God has great things in store for everyone, even those who come from humble beginnings. As a young boy, it was evident that Jesus was both fully God and fully human. The connection He had with His heavenly Father was so strong, it allowed Him to see God's plan for His life at a very early age. And He put that plan into action.

In His youth, Jesus sought to learn more about Scripture. So, He sat with a group of prominent religious leaders to listen, ask questions, and learn from them. This story reminds us of the importance of surrounding ourselves with people who challenge us to grow and who hold us accountable, especially as it relates to our faith. As we grow in our faith, it is important to find a community of believers who will come alongside us, encourage and strengthen our curiosity, and ensure we build our lives on His truth.

For many, faith is first learned through parents, grandparents, aunts, and uncles, especially during moments like the Passover festival, when stories, traditions, and beliefs are passed from one generation to the next. But not everyone begins their faith journey this way. Some discover faith later in life, without mentors to guide them, which makes it even more important to seek a community of believers who can help ground what we believe in truth, as revealed in Scripture. Whether faith is inherited or newly found, it grows best when it is shared, nurtured, and passed on, so what reaches the next generation is rooted firmly in God's word.

A Prayer to End

Dear God, thank You for telling us how Jesus grew in knowledge and wisdom, and how He honored You and His earthly family. Help us grow as He did by seeking Your truth with a loving heart, listening ears, and a deep desire to be closer to You. Surround us with people who encourage and teach us, and help us grow into the people You want us to become. Amen.

Bible References

Matthew 2 — The flight to Egypt and return to Nazareth
Luke 2 — Jesus' childhood and visit to the Temple at age twelve
Exodus 12 — The Passover remembrance

In the Year of Our Lord, ~AD 30

John the Baptist Prepares the Way

A Special Calling Before Birth

Before Jesus began His ministry of healing the sick, teaching the people, and encouraging the poor, God was working in someone who would help prepare the way for Jesus' work. That special person was John, later known as John the Baptist.

John's story began with a miracle. His parents, Zechariah and Elizabeth, had him very late in life. They were both faithful followers of God but were unable to have children of their own. One day, while Zechariah performed priestly duties in the Temple, an angel appeared to him and said, "Do not be afraid, Zechariah; your prayer has been heard. Your wife Elizabeth will bear you a son, and you are to call him John" (Luke 1:8-13). The angel Gabriel explained that John would be filled with the Holy Spirit, and he would help turn people's hearts back to God (Luke 1:15–16). John was born just as the angel foretold. As he grew, he dedicated his life to preparing the way for the Messiah.

Faithful and Reliant on God

John knew that to better help people, he had to live differently from those around him, so he moved away from the busyness of a "normal" life. He chose to live in the wilderness, where he wore clothes made of camel's hair and survived on a diet of locusts and wild honey (Matthew 3:4; Mark 1:6). He didn't do these things to be strange or weird; he did them to show people that when they are completely faithful and reliant on God, He provides and is worthy of our worship and praise.

In the years John spent in the wilderness, he studied Scriptures and listened closely for God's voice. He knew from the writings of the past that he was being prepared for something greater. As the prophet Isaiah once said, "In the wilderness prepare the way for the Lord; make straight in the desert a highway for our God" (Isaiah 40:3). God chose John to prepare the road for Jesus.

New Life Found on the Jordan

When the time came, John began preaching near the Jordan River. People from nearby towns gathered to hear him speak. His words were clear and bold: "Repent! Turn away from your sins and be baptized!" (Mark 1:4–5; Luke 3:3). He wasn't scared of the powerful leaders in the crowd nor afraid to speak the truth. He explained that everyone should get ready because the Savior of the world was coming soon (Matthew 3:11).

The crowd asked John what they should do in anticipation of the Lord's arrival. He told them to give generously, help those in need, to be just, and to not envy others (Luke 3:10–14). Those who believed and repented stepped into the river with John and were baptized as a sign that they wanted to leave their old ways behind and start fresh with God.

Even though John prepared the way for Jesus, he was always honest and made it clear to the people that he wasn't the Messiah. He said, "I baptize you with water. But one who is more powerful than I will come. He will baptize you with the Holy Spirit and fire" (Luke 3:16).

The Baptism of Jesus

One day, as John was baptizing people in the Jordan, Jesus approached him and asked to be baptized (Matthew 3:13; Mark 1:9). John immediately recognized the man standing in front of him as the Savior of the world. Initially, John felt unworthy to baptize Jesus and said, "I need to be baptized by you" (Matthew 3:14). But Jesus told him, "Let it be so now; it is proper for us to do this to fulfill all righteousness" (Matthew 3:15). After hearing Jesus say this, John obeyed and baptized Jesus.

As soon as Jesus was baptized, the heavens opened, and the Spirit of God came down like a dove and rested on Him. And a voice from heaven above said, "This is my Son, whom I love. With him I am well pleased" (Matthew 3:16–17).

In that moment, John completed what he had been called to do, preparing the way for the Lord to begin His ministry.

Why This Story Matters

John's life reminds us that even before we are born, God already has a plan and a purpose for each of us. But the question is, have our hearts been prepared to hear that plan? And when we do hear it, will we have the faith and courage to walk it out, trusting God will be right by our side no matter what He calls us to do?

Preparing our hearts is a daily process. It means allowing our thoughts, feelings, and desires to be open to God's will. As our hearts become aligned with Him, we can each play our part in pointing others to Jesus, just as John did. It may happen through an encouraging word, a listening ear, or simply the way we love others. God can use any of us to help prepare the way for someone else.

Like John, we must be willing to live differently and not get swept up in what everyone else around us is doing. When our hearts are changed and fully open to His will, we will be able to speak truth with boldness, walk in humility, and live with a joy and hope that draws others toward Jesus.

A Prayer to End

Dear God, thank You for John the Baptist and the way he prepared the world to meet King Jesus. Help us be like Him: brave, obedient, and focused on pointing others to You. Teach us to speak Your truth confidently, with love, and prepare our hearts daily. Thank You for giving each of us a part to play in Your greater story. Amen.

Bible References

Luke 1 — The birth of John foretold and fulfilled; the angel appears to Zechariah;
     John filled with the Holy Spirit
Isaiah 40 — Prepare the way for the Lord
Luke 3 — John's ministry in the wilderness
Matthew 3 — The baptism of Jesus

In the Year of Our Lord, ~AD 30

Jesus Tempted in the Wilderness

Preparing for the Work Ahead

After Jesus was baptized, instead of starting His public ministry right away, He was led by the Spirit into the wilderness. It was a place of isolation — hot, quiet, and lonely. There, Jesus didn't eat any food for forty days and forty nights. He fasted and prayed, spent time speaking with His heavenly Father, and prepared for the work ahead. This time spent refreshing His spirit was invaluable for what was yet to come.

Physically Weak but Faithful

In the Bible, the number forty often shows up during seasons of testing or preparation. The Israelites wandered in the desert for forty years, Noah waited in the ark through forty days of rain, and Moses was on Mount Sinai with God for forty days and nights. But unlike others who struggled while they waited, Jesus remained faithful in the wilderness.

Although He was hungry and physically weak, Jesus' spirit was strong. During this time, Satan, the enemy of God, tempted Him. His goal was to turn Jesus away from trusting God the Father and convince Him to place His trust in something lesser. Satan waited until Jesus was exhausted to approach Him, hoping that in a moment of weakness, He would give in. But Jesus was prepared (Matthew 4:1–11; Mark 1:12–13; Luke 4:1–13).

The First Temptation — Man Shall Not Live on Bread Alone

Knowing Jesus was hungry, Satan said, "If you are the Son of God, tell these stones to become bread" (Matthew 4:3). But Jesus answered with Scripture, "It is written, 'Man shall not live on bread alone, but on every word that comes from the mouth of God'" (Matthew 4:4, quoting Deuteronomy 8:3). Jesus knew trusting God's eternal truth was more important than satisfying His temporary hunger. He refused to be led by hunger when He had already chosen to be led by the Spirit of God.

The Second Temptation — Don't Put Your God to the Test

Next, Satan took Jesus to the highest point of the Temple in Jerusalem. There he said, "If you are the Son of God, throw yourself down. For it is written: 'He will command His angels … they will lift you up in their hands'" (Matthew 4:6). Satan tried to twist Scripture to lure

Jesus into testing God. But again, Jesus answered with truth: "It is also written: 'Do not put the Lord your God to the test'" (Matthew 4:7, quoting Deuteronomy 6:16). Jesus refused to use His power for show. He trusted that God's protection didn't need to be proven.

The Third Temptation — Only Worship God Almighty

Finally, Satan took Jesus to a high mountain and showed Him all the kingdoms of the world. He said, "All this I will give you, if you will bow down and worship me" (Matthew 4:9). Jesus had come to be King, but He would not take a shortcut. He answered, "Away from me, Satan! For it is written, 'Worship the Lord your God and serve Him only'" (Matthew 4:10, quoting Deuteronomy 6:13). At that moment, the devil left Jesus, and angels came to care for Him (Matthew 4:11).

Jesus didn't come into this world to sit on a throne built by man. He didn't need to. He had already been given authority over the world by His Father.

Why This Story Matters

God allowed Jesus to be tempted so He would fully understand how temptation impacts all of us. Jesus experienced what it felt like to be hungry, alone, and lied to, but He never gave in. And He didn't fight back with anger or pride. Instead, He used the word of God as His weapon to defeat the devil.

Even when Satan offered Jesus a way out, He overcame every temptation by standing firmly on God's truth, not by leaning on His own strength and understanding. Because Jesus faced every kind of temptation Himself and overcame it, we can call on His name in our time of need, and He will give us strength. His victory gives us a path forward, and His example teaches us how to stand strong.

Jesus also knew the importance of solitude, time away from noise and distraction, so He could hear His Father's voice clearly. Many times in the Bible, Jesus went to quiet places to recharge, reflect, and speak with His Father in prayer. Today, we need that same rhythm in our lives. Whether it is in the woods, at a park, or in a quiet corner of our own home, we grow stronger when we step away from the busyness of this world and draw close to God.

A Prayer to End

Dear God, thank You for allowing Jesus to face temptation so He could understand our struggles more deeply. We give You thanks for the angels who came and cared for Him after He passed each test. Help us be courageous like Jesus when we face trials or tough decisions.

Teach us to choose what is right and good, not what is easy or popular. Give us the patience and understanding to know Your truth, so we can rise up against those who oppose You — not with our emotions but with Your word. Amen.

Bible References

Matthew 3 — The baptism of Jesus
Matthew 4; Luke 4 — The temptation of Jesus
Deuteronomy 8 — Man lives by every word of God
Deuteronomy 6 — Do not test God, worship and serve Him only

Jesus Calls His First Disciples

The Busy Life in Galilee

The Sea of Galilee was busy with fishermen cleaning their nets and fish after a successful night out at sea. The next morning, the fisherman and townspeople walked back out to the shore to prepare for the day. Among them was Jesus, who had been teaching and healing the people in the community. Soon, news of His good works spread all over the region.

People in the crowd began to whisper, wondering how someone without any formal teaching could be so well versed in the Scriptures.

A Teacher Who Changed Everything

In the Jewish community, there was no one more respected than a practicing rabbi. To become one took more than just the ability to retain knowledge. You also had to prove you were holy and worthy enough to be called into the priesthood. Only a few who were formally educated had the opportunity to be trained under a master rabbi. Those who were accepted left their family and friends behind and devoted their entire lives to studying the Jewish Law. They spent months debating in the Temple courts and maintaining strict religious and dietary rules.

But then Jesus came. He changed everything.

He didn't look for students based on how gifted or smart they were. He didn't look for people who had perfect lives or had been studying Scripture for years. He stepped into everyday life and selected people no one expected.

A Fisher of Men

One morning, Jesus taught by the water's edge. As He spoke, the people pressed up to Him, eager to hear the word of God. As the crowds grew larger, Jesus saw two fishing boats by the shore and stepped into one so the people could better hear Him. He told the boat's owner, Simon Peter, to "Put the boat a little from shore," and Peter obeyed (Luke 5:3). Then Jesus sat down, allowing the soft waves to carry his message across the water. He spoke with wisdom and clarity and used words the people could understand.

When He finished teaching that day, He turned to Peter and the others and said, "Put out into deep water and let down the nets for a catch" (Luke 5:4). Peter briefly hesitated and replied, "We've worked hard all night and haven't caught anything. But because you say so, I will let down the nets" (Luke 5:5).

The fisherman let out their nets, and immediately, the water exploded with fish. Suddenly, there were so many fish in their nets that the nets began to break, and the boat started to sink because the weight of the fish was so great (Luke 5:6–7). Peter called out to his fishing partners, James and John, to help bring in their amazing catch (Luke 5:10). Soon, both boats struggled to stay afloat.

Once back on land, Peter fell to his knees and cried out to Jesus, "Go away from me, Lord, I am a sinful man!" (Luke 5:8). But Jesus assured him, "Don't be afraid; from now on you will fish for people" (Luke 5:10).

The Journey Begins

Right there on the water, their whole lives changed. Peter, James, Andrew, and John did something most people would never dream of doing: they left everything they owned behind and followed Jesus (Matthew 4:18–22).

They didn't know where the journey with Jesus would take them. But they knew He was special. None of the disciples were formally trained or mentored. Yet Jesus picked them anyway. By doing so, He shared with the world that no one had to be perfect. They only needed to have good hearts, an open mind, and a strong faith.

More Disciples Followed

This was just the beginning. Eventually, Jesus called eight other men to follow Him: Philip and Bartholomew; Thomas; Matthew the tax collector; James, the son of Alphaeus; Thaddaeus; Simon the Zealot; and Judas Iscariot, who would later betray Jesus (Matthew 10:2). Even though each man had a different background, Jesus invited them to be part of His inner circle, not because of their knowledge, but because they were willing to go wherever He led them.

Why This Story Matters

After hearing Jesus speak, many in the crowd were amazed and could sense there was something different about Him. When Jesus chose His disciples, He did so intentionally, seeing not only who they were, but who they could become. He selected men who would be open to His message, receptive to the truth, and willing to grow strong enough to carry the message forward to others.

Among those He chose was Simon Peter, later named just Peter. He had just finished a long night of work and had nothing to show for it. His nets were cleaned, the equipment put away, and he rested on shore with the others as he listened to Jesus teach. Then, Jesus asked him to return to the water and let down the nets once more. Though Peter hesitated, he chose obedience, and he was blessed because of it.

This story reminds us that Jesus meets us right where we are, just as we are, often in the ordinary places of life, like a fishing boat. When Jesus came to Galilee, He turned expectations upside down. Instead of choosing scholars or religious elites, He built His ministry with fishermen. That truth still stands today. We do not need to be perfect to follow or tell others about Jesus. He simply invites us to trust Him, step out in faith, and obey, even when nothing makes sense.

A Prayer to End

Dear God, thank You for sending us Jesus and showing us You are after our hearts and minds, not just interested in our rule-keeping. Give us confidence You can use each of us as we are to further Your Kingdom. Grant us wisdom and strength to feel Your presence and to act on it. Help us be ready, willing, and able to say yes when You call. And when we speak of who You are, give us the words that will reach the hearts of others. Amen.

Bible References

Luke 5 — The miraculous catch and calling of the first disciples
Matthew 4 — Jesus calls Peter, Andrew, James, and John
Matthew 10 — The full list of the twelve apostles

Jesus' First Miracle — Water into Wine

The Celebration Begins

Not long after Jesus called His disciples together, He and His mother, Mary, were invited to attend a large wedding in Cana, a little town in Galilee (John 2:1). Weddings in biblical times were huge events that brought the whole community together to celebrate. Certain wedding traditions required the host to house and feed the guests, attend carefully to their needs, and oversee a celebration that could last several days.

The wedding Jesus attended made history as the first place He performed a miracle, but only a few people witnessed it. There was no fanfare, and He didn't try to draw attention to Himself. He only wanted to bring honor to the wedding hosts (John 2:10-11).

The Problem No One Saw Coming

The wedding celebration was in full swing — guests danced, children laughed, tables were decorated with flowers and jars of perfume, and there was plenty of food and drink. But soon, an unexpected problem arose: there was no more wine (John 2:3).

In those days, not having enough wine to last the entire wedding celebration wasn't just embarrassing; it could bring great shame to the family hosting the event. If they ran out of wine too soon, the guests might think the hosts were not prepared or were of poor means.

Whispers of this problem began to spread through the crowd, and Mary quickly turned to Jesus and said, "They have no more wine" (John 2:3). She didn't demand anything from Jesus, nor did she panic. She simply shared the problem with the person she trusted most: her Son.

Jesus replied with gentleness and honesty, "Woman, why do you involve me? My hour has not yet come" (John 2:4). He said this because it was not time for Him to reveal who He really was to the world. Mary trusted Jesus would do what was in the best interest of those in attendance. She looked at the wedding attendants and quietly said, "Do whatever he tells you" (John 2:5).

Jesus' First Miracle

Six large empty stone jars were nearby, each used for ceremonial washing, a special religious practice that required priests to wash and clean themselves before worship service or eating meals. The jars held up to twenty to thirty gallons each and weren't meant to hold wine but cleansing water (John 2:6).

Jesus told the servants to take the jars and fill them with water. They obeyed without hesitation, even though they were likely confused. Still, they did as they were told and filled each jar to the brim (John 2:7).

Then Jesus said, "Now draw some out and take it to the master of the banquet." The servants did just as He asked (John 2:8).

When the master of the wedding banquet tasted the water that had been turned into wine, he was amazed. He didn't know where the wine came from, but he could tell it was excellent. He called the groom over and said, "Everyone brings out the choice wine first and then the cheaper wine after the guests have had too much to drink; but you have saved the best till now" (John 2:9–10).

The wedding guests had no idea what had happened, but Jesus' disciples and the wedding attendants knew (John 2:9, 11). He honored the host family and protected them from embarrassment and shame on their very special day.

Jesus didn't perform this miracle in public to gain favor. He simply gave the people a small glimpse of the many wonders He would do throughout His ministry, eventually offering salvation to the whole world.

Why This Story Matters

This story shows us Jesus cares about the little things that are often overlooked, as well as the big miracles that steal the headlines. He wasn't obligated to help the wedding hosts, but He helped them anyway. He noticed someone in need and responded quietly and compassionately, restoring joy to a celebration that was about to be spoiled. This story is a great reminder that Jesus sees our needs even if no one else does, and He steps in to help us, bringing hope right when we need it most.

But there is more happening here than a single act of kindness. Even the details of this miracle carry meaning.

The six stone water jars were used for ceremonial washing, part of the religious tradition of the Jews. Before entering the Temple or serving in religious duties, priests washed themselves with water in an outward attempt to appear clean before God. But these rituals were created by man, and they could only make a person clean on the outside.

At Cana, Jesus turned those jars into something completely new. He changed water meant for external cleansing into wine, a symbol of His blood that would one day be poured out for the forgiveness of sins. In that moment, Jesus showed He did not come to continue old rituals, but to fulfill them. Water can only wash the body, but His blood cleanses the heart. He alone has the power to make us truly clean, not because of who we are or what we do, but because of who He is.

A Prayer to End

Dear God, thank You for reminding us there isn't any detail about our lives You are not familiar with. Just as Jesus stepped in and helped at the wedding, we know You see our needs and give us what we need when we need it, not always when we ask for it. Teach us to obey like the wedding attendants, when You ask, that we too will act. Help us trust You, even when we don't understand how You're working for our good. Amen.

Bible References

John 2 — Jesus turns water into wine at Cana

In the Year of Our Lord, ~AD 30

Jesus Clears the Temple

The Place of Prayer and Worship Forgotten

Shortly after Jesus began His public ministry, He traveled to Jerusalem to prepare and take part in the city's Passover festival (John 2:13). The Passover celebration was a special time. Jewish families from all over the region came together to worship and remember when God sent Moses to Egypt to rescue His people and how He protected them from the tenth plague, the angel of death (Exodus 12:12–14).

When Jesus entered the Temple courts, the place that was meant to be a holy sanctuary for prayer and worship, He saw what was happening inside the Temple, and it broke His heart. The Temple had been turned into a marketplace. Instead of being filled with songs and God's presence, it was now filled with noise and chaos. Buyers and sellers came together and haggled over prices. There were merchant tables displayed everywhere showcasing goods for sale: clothing, food, and even animals. Live animals such as sheep, doves, and cattle were allowed inside the Temple of God (John 2:14).

How Did the Temple Become a Marketplace?

Animal sacrifice was part of the Jewish religious tradition. Jews believed the blood of animals washed away the sins of the person or family who offered the sacrifice (Leviticus 4:20). People from faraway lands traveled to Jerusalem to visit the Temple. It was already difficult for a traveler to make their way to the Holy City — they had to deal with rough terrain, heat, snakes, and much more. To make the trip with live animals was even more challenging. So, the local priests and merchants set up a system where people could purchase animals once they arrived. That might sound helpful, but their intentions weren't good. Instead of showing genuine concern for the people, they established a business focused on profits and greed.

The merchants overcharged travelers for the animals needed for sacrifice, taking advantage of those who came to Jerusalem to worship. Even though the priests were aware of what was happening, they sat idly by and allowed this unjust practice to continue because they received a portion of the profits.

Alongside the merchants were a group of men known as money changers. They oversaw the process of exchanging Roman coins for special Temple currency, which was the only money accepted for purchases made inside the Temple courts (Matthew 21:12). Roman coins were considered unclean because they displayed images of emperors, so visitors were required to exchange their money before worship.

Rather than offering fair exchanges, the money changers exploited this system for personal gain. Their rates were often dishonest and unfair (Mark 11:15). For example, a traveler might hand over a Roman coin worth five shekels but only receive three shekels of Temple currency, with the money changers keeping the difference as profit.

Jesus Pushes Back

When Jesus saw such corruption taking place, He refused to stand by and let it continue. He took action. Jesus made a whip out of cords to drive the animals out of the courtyards, and He overturned the tables where the money changers did business, scattering their coins all over the Temple floor (John 2:15).

He said with a loud, bold voice, "It is written: 'My house will be called a house of prayer,' but you are making it 'a den of robbers'" (Matthew 21:13, quoting Isaiah 56:7 and Jeremiah 7:11).

The Jewish leaders were furious and confronted Him, demanding to know by what authority He acted in such a way (Matthew 21:23). Jesus answered them with a statement they didn't understand: "Destroy this temple, and I will raise it again in three days" (John 2:19). His words were absurd to them; it had taken forty-six years to build the Temple they oversaw. But Jesus was not talking about stone walls. He was speaking about His own body, the true dwelling place of God with His people, and the resurrection that was to come (John 2:20–21).

Why Were the Religious Leaders Upset?

The religious leaders in charge of the Temple were enraged. Not only had Jesus interrupted their rituals, but He had exposed their wicked money-making schemes. They were using the Temple — the very house of God — for personal profit and power, and they did not like being called out. By clearing out the Temple, Jesus challenged their authority. But His courageous act wasn't met with humility and reflection. Instead, He became a focus of their scorn. Because they feared His influence with the common people, the leaders began to plot ways to stop Him (Mark 11:18).

Why This Story Matters

This story reminds us that Jesus cares deeply about people and the purity of our worship. He sees past our outward appearances and looks directly at the motives of our hearts. Sometimes we need to be strong, like Jesus, and speak up when we see things we know are not right, not to cause trouble, but to bring about truth, peace, and justice.

Worship should never be about profit, personal gain, or seeking status. The Temple had become a place of greed and dishonesty, and Jesus would not allow it. He stood up for what was right, even when those in positions of authority wouldn't, and it brought Him powerful enemies.

When Jesus responded, "Destroy this temple, and I will raise it again in three days" (John 2:19), He announced something far greater than repairs to a building. He spoke about the fulfillment of God's promise: that through His death and resurrection, the true meeting place between God and His people would be found in Him. Yet the religious leaders, the ones who claimed to know the Scriptures best, did not understand what He meant. They were focused on rules, routines, and their own positions of power. Their hearts were not centered on God, so they missed the One standing right in front of them. It is a reminder that if our faith becomes all about outward practices, we may miss Jesus pointing us toward faith that is genuine, compassionate, and active.

A Prayer to End

Dear God, thank You for showing us that Your house and our hearts should be places of worship, not of selfish gain. Take away anything in our lives that keeps us from truly loving, praising, and honoring You. Give us wisdom to care more about what matters to You than what pleases the world. Thank You for Your example of what it looks like to fight for the weak, poor, and disadvantaged. Amen.

Bible References

John 2 — Jesus clears the Temple
Exodus 12 — The first Passover
Leviticus 4 — Sacrifice for the forgiveness of sins
Matthew 21 — Jesus confronts corruption in the Temple
Mark 11 — The religious leaders oppose Jesus
Isaiah 56 — A house of prayer for all nations
Jeremiah 7 — God's house turned into a den of robbers

Pause & Reflect — Invitation

Jesus Came for Everyone

Jesus did not begin His ministry in places of comfort, status, or religious approval. He stepped first into the outskirts of society, into towns and homes where the poor, the sick, and those who had been dismissed lived. He went to people others avoided, intentionally placing Himself among those who had been pushed aside or looked down upon. Jesus came to heal the broken and restore the hurting, reminding the world that God had not forgotten them, and inviting them into a new life as part of His family. As He said, "For the Son of Man came to seek and to save the lost" (Luke 19:10).

From the beginning, God knew we could not rescue ourselves. The religious leaders of the time had lost sight of God's heart, placing rules above people and tradition above compassion. So God sent Jesus, not just for a select few, but for all. Jesus came to reopen the way to the Father, offering grace instead of judgment and mercy instead of exclusion. There were no barriers to His invitation, no qualifications to earn His love.

Jesus also understands that believing this is not always easy. We may doubt. We may hesitate. We may feel unworthy or too broken to belong. Still, Jesus waits patiently. He meets us where we are and welcomes us as we come, not asking us to fix ourselves first, but inviting us into His family just as we are.

Memory Verse

"I am the way and the truth and the life. No one comes to the Father except through me." — John 14:6

Questions to Consider

Is there something causing us to believe Jesus did not come for us?

Is there something in our past we believe Jesus could never forgive, something that would exclude us from His eternal family?

A Prayer to End

Dear Jesus, thank You for inviting all of us to Your table, no matter our past, our failures, or our doubts. Help us release the lies that tell us we are unworthy of Your love. Give us the courage to believe Your grace truly is for everyone, including us. Teach us to rest in the truth that You came to heal the broken, and that means You came for all of us. Amen.

In the Year of Our Lord, ~AD 30

Born Again — Nicodemus Meets with Jesus

A Visitor in the Middle of the Night

Jesus had just stood up to those in authority who allowed the Temple to be misused, flipping over tables and driving out the merchants who made God's house into a place of business (John 2:13–16). People all over the town were talking about Him. They saw His miraculous works performed during the Passover festival (John 2:23), and the crowds that followed Him grew bigger and bigger.

Many Pharisees didn't understand or accept Jesus' activities in the community. But Nicodemus was different. He sensed there was something special about Jesus — the way He taught the masses and the miracles He performed pointed to something greater.

Nicodemus was a Pharisee, one of many religious leaders who lived in Jerusalem. He was also a member of the Sanhedrin, a powerful group of men that helped guide the observance of Jewish laws and decision-making (John 3:1). Nicodemus spent his entire life studying Scripture and following God's commands. He knew the Torah, the Jewish Scriptures, and the laws well, yet he sensed something was missing from his religion. The recent events surrounding Jesus stirred his curiosity.

Even though the other Pharisees were skeptical, Nicodemus felt compelled to find out for himself who Jesus really was. But instead of going to see Jesus during the day when the town was alive with people, Nicodemus went to Him in the middle of the night (John 3:2). He was probably nervous about what others in the community might think if they saw him meeting with Jesus face-to-face. Or maybe he just wanted to speak with Him privately. Whatever the reason, when Nicodemus arrived, Jesus welcomed him.

Honest Questions

Nicodemus began by saying, "Rabbi, we know that you are a teacher who has come from God. For no one could perform the signs you are doing if God were not with him" (John 3:2).

Nicodemus' words seemed flattering, but Jesus knew the real reason he had come to visit Him. It was deeper than the words Nicodemus spoke; Jesus knew he wasn't there to pay

Him compliments. Nicodemus' heart was filled with big questions, questions he needed answered. Knowing this, Jesus responded even before Nicodemus had a chance to probe further.

"Very truly I tell you, no one can see the kingdom of God unless they are born again" (John 3:3).

This caught Nicodemus completely off guard, and he was confused. "How can someone be born when they are old?" he asked. "Surely they cannot enter a second time into their mother's womb to be born!" (John 3:4).

Spiritual Rebirth

Jesus explained, "No one can enter the kingdom of God unless they are born of water and the Spirit. Flesh gives birth to flesh, but the Spirit gives birth to spirit" (John 3:5–6). His message about birth had nothing to do with a physical rebirth. He was speaking about something more meaningful — a spiritual rebirth.

Still, all of this was hard for Nicodemus to understand. He spent his entire life following rules and memorizing Scripture. Now Jesus showed him something completely different — that following rules would never allow him to build a meaningful relationship with God.

The Great Invitation

God's word makes this clear, something so important that it's still remembered thousands of years later: "For God so loved the world that he gave his one and only Son, that whoever believes in him shall not perish but have eternal life" (John 3:16).

Scripture goes on to reveal a powerful truth: that God's love was for all mankind. When we decide to put our faith in the One who was sent, the Holy Spirit comes over us, like purifying water, refreshing our minds and souls so our hearts are prepared to receive Him.

Nicodemus may not have fully understood all he heard, but meeting Jesus planted the seed of all that was possible through faith in Him.

Why This Story Matters

This story reminds us of the importance of listening to our hearts and not being influenced by others, especially when we know they are not right. Nicodemus knew there was something special when he saw Jesus. Even though others were skeptical, he sought Him out to learn more about the truth He was proclaiming.

Jesus also shared how we are all offered the opportunity to be part of God's family. This invitation to start anew can't be earned; it's received by faith in Jesus Christ because of God's grace, mercy, and love for us. That's what being "born again" means: accepting Jesus into our lives and letting the Holy Spirit guide us.

And just as Nicodemus did, as we grow closer to Jesus, it's normal and good to bring our questions, problems, and worries to Him. Jesus can handle it. He wants us to lean on Him. He invites us to seek Him so our relationship can grow stronger. In those quiet moments of prayer when we draw near to Him, He meets us there with wisdom, love, and compassion.

A Prayer to End

Dear Jesus, thank You, we don't need to be perfect to be part of God's family; we only need to have faith in You. Each day, help us remember, even when others make us feel like we are not enough, we are perfectly made in Your image. Help us recognize and strengthen the spiritual gifts You've placed within us so we can make a difference in this world. Amen.

Bible References
John 2 — Jesus clears the Temple
John 3 — Jesus and Nicodemus, born again

The Woman at the Well — A Story of Living Water

Resting at Jacob's Well

After a long day of preaching and teaching, Jesus decided to rest. He and His disciples came to a town in Samaria called Sychar, near the plot of ground Jacob had given to his son, Joseph. Jacob's well was located there (John 4:5–6). This was the same Jacob we read about in Scripture, whose son Joseph received a colorful coat as a gift and was later sold into slavery by his brothers (Genesis 37:3, 27–28).

Jesus, weary from His journey, sat beside the well while His disciples went into the city to buy food and supplies. As He rested, He noticed a Samaritan woman approaching alone to draw water.

A Chance Encounter

As the woman came near, Jesus said to her, "Will you give me a drink?" (John 4:7). The woman was surprised and replied that Jews were not supposed to speak to Samaritans. At that time, the Jewish people looked down on Samaritans and considered them unclean because they were only partly Jewish.

Here is a bit more background: About a thousand years ago, during the time of the judges, pride and arrogance within Israel's leadership caused the kingdom to split into two nations. Judah became the Southern Kingdom, and Israel became the Northern Kingdom. The Northern Kingdom was frequently invaded by foreign nations, such as the Assyrians, Moabites, and Philistines (2 Kings 17). After many of these invasions, some foreigners stayed behind, intermarried with the Israelites, and started new lives in the land. Their descendants became the Samaritans.

Because of these mixed marriages and the foreign gods that were introduced, the Jews of the Southern Kingdom believed the Samaritans of the north had corrupted their faith (Ezra 4). They viewed them as impure and unworthy to worship in the Temple in Jerusalem. As a result, the Samaritans built their own place of worship on Mount Gerizim (John 4:20).

The Offer of Living Water

This is why the Samaritan woman was shocked that Jesus, a Jewish man, was willing to speak with her. She didn't realize Jesus saw her as someone deeply loved by God, not as someone to avoid.

He told her, "If you knew the gift of God and who it is that asks you for a drink, you would have asked him and he would have given you living water" (John 4:10). She was confused at first; Jesus had no bucket, no rope. How could He offer water? He explained the water He offered would satisfy her thirst forever. He was speaking of eternal life, the new life God gives through faith in Him (John 4:13–14).

Intrigued by His words, the woman said, "Sir, give me this water so that I won't get thirsty and have to keep coming here to draw water" (John 4:15). In response, Jesus told her to go and call her husband. She replied that she didn't have a husband. With compassion, Jesus confirmed she was right — she had no husband now, though she had been married five times before (John 4:16–18). Jesus didn't reveal these details to embarrass her, but to help her face the truth about her life and begin the process of healing.

Uncertainty Around Worship

The woman then asked Jesus a question about the proper place to worship. "Sir," she said, "I can see you are a prophet. Our ancestors worshiped on this mountain, but you Jews claim the place where we must worship is in Jerusalem" (John 4:19–20). Because the religious leaders had made the Samaritans feel unwelcome in Jerusalem, many were confused about where and how to worship. Jesus looked at her with compassion and told her the truth: a time was coming when worship would not be limited to a place, because true worship comes from the heart (John 4:21–24).

Up until Jesus' arrival, generations of Jewish leaders believed righteousness came through strict obedience to the law. There were more than six hundred Jewish commandments, known as the Mitzvot, which covered every part of daily life. But what was meant to guide people toward God had become a burden — a checklist of rituals rather than a relationship. That's why God sent His Son. Jesus came to bring eternal life, to show that God truly desires genuine worship … not performance, but devotion.

Why This Story Matters

Jesus came to turn the world upside down. True worship comes from the heart, through Spirit and truth, not through a location, a building, or religious tradition. God cannot be confined to a temple or a church. He desires a relationship with His people, not religion based on rules and appearances.

The woman at the well expected judgment from Jesus but received compassion instead. She was alone at the well in the heat of the day, likely avoiding others because of shame. Yet this Samaritan woman was the first person Jesus openly revealed His identity to during His earthly ministry. He didn't reveal Himself to the Pharisees, the Sadducees, or the religious leaders, but to her. Jesus didn't condemn her; He offered her grace, love, and a fresh start, welcoming her into His eternal family.

Like the Samaritan woman, many of us carry regret or feel unworthy of love and forgiveness. We may think we are too broken, too far gone, or too imperfect to matter to God. Jesus meets us right where we are. He doesn't turn us away. He invites us to lay down our burdens and receive His living water, His mercy, His forgiveness, and His new life.

A Prayer to End

Dear Jesus, thank You for being a humble and compassionate King. Thank You for seeing the good in us, even when we struggle to see it ourselves. Help us remove the weight of shame and fear the enemy tries to place on us. Lift us up in Your strength so we can live the life You have planned for us, a life full of purpose, peace, and hope. Help us rest in Your love and walk boldly in Your grace. Amen.

Bible References

Genesis 37 — Jacob gives Joseph the colorful coat; Joseph sold into slavery by his brothers
2 Kings 17 — Assyrians invade Israel and settle in Samaria, forming the Samaritan people
Ezra 4 — Samaritans oppose rebuilding the temple after the exile
John 4 — Jesus meets the Samaritan woman and offers her living water

In the Year of Our Lord, ~AD 30

Jesus Rejected in His Hometown

Jesus Comes Home to Nazareth

After Jesus started His ministry, preaching, healing, and performing miracles in towns throughout Galilee, He returned to the area where He grew up, the small town of Nazareth (Luke 4:16). The people in the community knew Him well. They had seen Him grow from a child to an adult, watched Him memorize Scriptures and the Torah, and seen Him train to be a carpenter under the watchful eye of His earthly father, Joseph. Now Jesus was back home, this time not as a young, curious boy, but as a wise teacher, a rabbi with great knowledge and power.

One Sabbath, Jesus walked to the synagogue, a Jewish church, just like He had done many times before as a young man (Luke 4:16). This time, though, the religious leaders asked Him to come forward so He could read aloud from the Scriptures.

Reading from the Scroll of Isaiah

Jesus walked up and stood confidently in front of those in attendance as a religious attendant handed Him the scroll of the prophet Isaiah. He unrolled the scroll and focused on a special passage about the coming Messiah (Luke 4:17).

"The Spirit of the Lord is on me, because he has anointed me to proclaim good news to the poor. He has sent me to proclaim freedom for the prisoners and recovery of sight for the blind, to set the oppressed free, to proclaim the year of the Lord's favor" (Luke 4:18–19, quoting from Isaiah 61:1–2).

Then Jesus did something that caught everyone off guard. After He finished reading, He rolled up the scroll and gave it back to the religious attendant standing beside Him and sat down. As He did so, each person's eyes were fixed on Him. Breaking the silence, He said, "Today this Scripture is fulfilled in your hearing" (Luke 4:20–21).

Jesus Dismissed

At first, the people were amazed at the power and confidence in His words. They hadn't heard anyone in Jesus' position teach like He did, in a way that drew them closer to God. But then someone in the crowd began to whisper, "Isn't this Joseph's son?" And then others joined in. "We know His family. How could He say something like that?" Their amazement quickly turned into doubt and resentment (Luke 4:22).

Even before the whispers started, Jesus knew exactly what they were thinking and how their hearts were changing. He responded to them and said, "No prophet is accepted in his hometown" (Luke 4:24).

Then He reminded the people of two powerful stories from Scripture — the widow in Zarephath and Naaman, the Syrian (1 Kings 17:9–24; 2 Kings 5:1–14). Neither of them was Jewish, yet their faithful response to God through the prophets Elijah and Elisha changed their lives. In both cases, God's miracles and blessings touched two people who were not Israelites. By sharing these stories, Jesus made a bold statement: God honors faith, not heritage (Luke 4:25–27). He told his listeners how two Gentiles, people not part of the Jewish community, had acknowledged and responded to God's power, while many in Israel, including those with Him that day, had not.

This truth offended those in the crowd. Instead of Jesus' words humbling their hearts, His words made them angry. He directly challenged their assumption that they were God's chosen people. Many thought, "How dare He suggest God would bless an outsider before us!"

Pushed Out of Town

Jesus, the Savior of the world, had arrived in fulfillment of Isaiah's prophecy. But instead of celebrating His appearance, the crowd turned on Him and tried to kill Him. The people, in an act of defiance, rose up and drove Him out of the synagogue, took Him to the edge of a cliff, and intended to throw Him off (Luke 4:28–29). Jesus, however, calmly turned toward the hostile crowd, walked right through the chaos, and quietly left town (Luke 4:30).

Jesus came to Nazareth to bring a message of truth, healing, and hope, but His own community, the people who had watched Him grow up, rejected Him.

Why This Story Matters

When Jesus stood up to read from the scroll in the synagogue, He knew His words might challenge and even offend those listening. Still, He spoke with courage, trusting His Father to give Him the strength and confidence He needed. The people who should have known Him best did not recognize Him, and they rejected Him. Even more, they turned away from the very Scriptures that pointed to who He truly was.

Yet rejection in His hometown did not stop Jesus from moving forward. He continued to trust His Father's plan and to love people faithfully every step of the way. In the same way, when we choose a new life in Christ, some may struggle to believe the change within us is real. They may focus on who we once were instead of who God is shaping us to become. But it is not the opinions of others that define us. Jesus does.

When old doubts or past regrets try to resurface, we can lift our heads with confidence, knowing we are a new creation in Him. He has broken the chains of our past and invites us to walk boldly into the future He has prepared for us. Following God does not mean life will always be easy, but we can rest in this promise: God walks closely with the faithful.

A Prayer to End

Dear God, give us the confidence to always speak truth, and may it come from the heart. Help us remain faithful to You, especially when it's tough. Give us opportunities to meet others where they are and to love them for who they are. Let us live lives filled with joy, encouragement, peace, and love, so the good seen in us by others is a direct reflection of who You are. Amen.

Bible References

Luke 4 — Jesus rejected in Nazareth
Isaiah 61 — The prophecy Jesus read in the synagogue
1 Kings 17 — Elijah and the widow of Zarephath
2 Kings 5 — Naaman healed by Elisha

In the Year of Our Lord, ~AD 31

Faithfulness Lowered and Stretched

The Overcrowded House in Capernaum

Jesus came to Capernaum, and the town buzzed with anticipation as word of His arrival quickly spread (Mark 2:1). His first stop was at a small, unassuming house near the town center. Before long, the house overflowed with people; men and women jostled for position, standing shoulder-to-shoulder, leaning in through doorways and windows, all hoping to hear Jesus speak and see the One who had the power to perform miracles (Luke 5:17).

As the crowd grew, four men from a forgotten part of the city carried their friend on a dusty old mat toward the huge gathering. The man had been paralyzed for many years. He could not walk, find work, or care for himself. But when his friends heard Jesus was in town, they were filled with renewed hope — a hope that inspired them to keep moving forward. They had faith in Jesus and believed that if they got their friend to Him, something amazing would happen.

By the time they arrived, the crowd surrounding the house was so big that there was no way for them to get through the front door. But these friends were motivated and didn't give up. They climbed onto the rooftop, carefully dug a hole through the clay and straw roof, and with ropes and sure hands, slowly lowered their friend into the house, right at the feet of Jesus (Mark 2:4).

Everyone inside the house froze when they saw what was happening. Jesus gazed up at the men on the roof, then looked down at the man now at His feet. He smiled and, in a gentle voice, said, "Son, your sins are forgiven" (Mark 2:5).

Gasps came from every corner of the room. Some Pharisees stood nearby and thought to themselves, "Who is this fellow who speaks blasphemy? Who can forgive sins but God alone?" (Luke 5:21).

Jesus was aware of what they thought and asked if it was easier to tell someone their sins were forgiven or to tell them to get up and walk. He also let the crowd know the Son of Man had the authority to forgive sins. After saying this, He looked at the paralyzed man and instructed him to get off his mat and to go home (Mark 2:9–11). The room fell silent as the man slowly sat up. Then, with strength that had left him long ago, he rose to his feet, rolled up his mat, and walked out the door (Luke 5:25).

The crowd stood in awe as he walked past them. Some people reached out to him; others cried. But most praised God in heaven for what they had just witnessed (Mark 2:12).

A Miracle Performed on the Sabbath

Soon after, Jesus was teaching in a synagogue when a man with a shriveled hand stood aside hoping to be healed (Mark 3:1). It was the Sabbath, and the Pharisees, who added their own man-made laws to God's commands, had added a rule that no one could be healed on the Sabbath. They considered that work, and the Sabbath was only meant for rest and worship (Luke 6:7).

They observed Jesus closely to see if He would heal the man. Jesus knew their thoughts and asked, "Which is lawful on the Sabbath: to do good or to do evil, to save life or to destroy it?" (Luke 6:9).

No one said a word.

Then Jesus told the man, "Stretch out your hand." The man obeyed, and his hand was completely healed (Mark 3:5). The people knew they had just seen a miracle. The awesome power, compassion, and love of the One God sent were on full display.

But instead of rejoicing over what they had just witnessed, the Pharisees were angry. Not only had Jesus broken their man-made rule, but He challenged their authority once again. His teaching exposed how their faith had become focused on control and tradition rather than on love and mercy.

After this encounter, the Pharisees began to plot ways to stop Jesus (Mark 3:6).

Why This Story Matters

The religious leaders watched from the shadows, waiting for Jesus to make a mistake so they could accuse Him. Yet the true mistake was their misunderstanding of what God's law was meant to accomplish. They had elevated rules above mercy. Jesus saw through their hardened thinking and acted in faith. Sometimes doing what is right means challenging the status quo. In both of these stories, Jesus makes it clear that love and healing matter more to God than human approval or rigid expectations.

These stories remind us that God cares far more about people's hearts than about religious traditions. Jesus did not come to impress rule keepers. He came to bring healing, mercy, and restoration to the sick, the lost, and the oppressed. He saw the faith of a few determined friends and the quiet hope of a man living with pain, and He responded with compassion, even though it offended the Pharisees and brought trouble upon Himself.

In today's world, it is easy to go along with the crowd and avoid drawing attention or causing discomfort. But when we walk with Christ and allow His Spirit to guide us, He gives us the courage and the words to do what is right and to speak up in faith, even in the face of opposition. When we live this way, we step into the life God intended for us, a life that reflects His love, goodness, and truth, and helps others experience Him through the way we live each day.

A Prayer to End

Dear Jesus, give us overwhelming faith and compassion like the men who lowered their friend to You through the roof. And give us unrelenting courage like the man with the shriveled hand, who stood in hope, day after day, even when others watched in doubt. Let us remain focused on doing what's right rather than what's allowed. And thank You for seeing those in need and bringing Your healing power. Amen.

Bible References

Mark 2 — Jesus heals the paralyzed man
Luke 5 — Faith of the friends and forgiveness of sins
Mark 3 — Jesus heals the man with the shriveled hand
Luke 6 — Confrontation about healing on the Sabbath

In the Year of Our Lord, ~AD 31

Matthew the Tax Collector — Called by Jesus

The Man Behind the Tax Booth

In the busy city of Capernaum, there was a wealthy Jewish man named Matthew, whom most people despised. They considered him a thief and a criminal, but not in the usual sense. You see, Matthew was a tax collector, a position that drew hate from many of his fellow Jews who lived in his community (Matthew 9:9).

Back then, the Roman Empire ruled over many nations it had conquered, including Israel. The cost to oversee this expanding empire required the ability to control cities, livestock, money, and even people. And when it came to money, Rome needed a lot of it. So, Roman leaders collected funds by taxing people's lands, which allowed them to pay for more soldiers, equipment, and government officials needed to maintain and further expand the Roman Empire.

This financial system required foreign nations that were part of the Roman Empire to collect taxes from their citizens and then send the money back to Rome. The Romans hired local Jewish men to oversee this operation. To secure these jobs, men like Matthew paid Roman officials money to earn the right to win tax contracts. Then, the tax collectors set up tax booths near busy marketplaces or city entryways and collected money from their own people to earn it back.

Rome taxed people's homes, land, crops, and livestock. Foreign travelers even had to pay taxes for using roads. Fishermen like Peter and Andrew not only had to pay taxes on their boats, but every catch they hauled in was counted and taxed, too. The more they caught, the more Rome collected.

Then there was the actual payment of taxes, which came in many forms: silver or gold coins, or sometimes by substituting goods, such as wheat, for money. It all depended on what someone had. And worst of all, some tax collectors took more than what was required, keeping a little extra for themselves (Luke 3:12–13).

So, while it was difficult for many in the community to feed their families, in contrast, tax collectors lived in big homes, ate good food, and were guarded by Roman soldiers. People saw them as traitors who worked for the enemy. Even the religious leaders believed tax collectors were unclean and would purposely cross the street to avoid walking by them.

However, Jesus still noticed Matthew.

Given an Invitation to Follow

One day, Jesus passed by Matthew's booth, but He wasn't angry and didn't spit at him as others did. Instead, Jesus stopped. He looked at Matthew, directly into his eyes, and said, "Follow me" (Matthew 9:9).

That was the extent of His invitation. He didn't give a long speech about Matthew's actions or how he should do better. Just two words. Just a simple request. In that moment, Matthew left everything he knew behind — his job, his money, his security — and followed Jesus (Luke 5:28).

Later that evening, Matthew held a big dinner at his home to honor Jesus and invited other people from the community, people the religious leaders considered "sinners" (Luke 5:29). They all sat together at the table, listening to Jesus tell stories, laughing, and asking Him questions. For the first time, these "sinners" didn't feel ashamed or unworthy. They started to believe that, maybe, their lives actually mattered.

The Pharisees Offended

The Pharisees were religious leaders who carefully followed God's law but often focused more on rules than love and mercy. They saw the group of men gathering at Matthew's house and were deeply offended. "Why does your teacher eat with tax collectors and sinners?" they asked Jesus' disciples (Matthew 9:11). Jesus heard their comments and answered them Himself: "It is not the healthy who need a doctor, but the sick. I have not come to call the righteous, but sinners to repentance" (Luke 5:31–32).

The Pharisees spent each morning and night studying the Scriptures. Over time, they added more rules and traditions, believing that following rules made them holy. They eventually lost sight of God's purpose behind the commandments: love, mercy, and justice (Micah 6:8). Jesus understood the error in the Pharisees' thinking. So when He sat with Matthew for dinner, He wasn't breaking the law like the Pharisees accused Him of. No, He was correcting their understanding of the law.

Why This Story Matters

Matthew didn't intend to live a sinful life; he made a living doing what made sense to him at the time. He chose a path that provided money, status, and security. But what he gained in wealth, he lost in building community, connection, and peace. People despised him for the choices he made, and deep down, he knew something was missing.

That's when Jesus entered his life. He didn't just see Matthew as a tax collector. He saw a man with a tired heart who was ready for change. When Jesus invited him to "Follow me," it was more than a call; it was the answer to a longing Matthew could not put into words. It was a fresh beginning, an opportunity to center his life on something far greater than the power, status, and wealth he once pursued, things that had never truly brought him peace or fulfillment.

This story reminds us that no one is ever too far gone for Jesus to accept them. No matter how many mistakes we've made or how the world views us, Jesus sees the heart inside each of us. He welcomes each of us to be part of His eternal family.

A Prayer to End

Dear Jesus, when the world tries to make us believe we're not good enough, remind us that You came for people like Matthew, people like us, who are tired of living by our own rules and understanding and ready to follow You. Help those who feel unworthy, forgotten, or dismissed know You are never far away, waiting with open arms, ready to forgive, restore, and lead them into a new beginning. Amen.

Bible References

Matthew 9 — Jesus calls Matthew
Luke 3 — John teaches tax collectors
Luke 5 — Matthew follows Jesus and hosts a banquet
Micah 6 — God desires mercy, not empty religion

The Sermon on the Mount

Jesus' Early Ministry

Not long after Jesus was rejected in His hometown, He heard disturbing news: King Herod had thrown John the Baptist into prison for speaking out against the king's unlawful marriage to Herodias, his brother's wife (Matthew 14:3–4). Before his arrest, John the Baptist prepared the way for Jesus, commanding the people in the region to turn back to God and repent. But now, in jail, his voice was silenced. Jesus sensed it was time to take the reins and begin to share the message of God's Kingdom Himself (Matthew 4:12, 17).

Seven hundred years earlier, the prophet Isaiah wrote that someone special would come to Israel one day to bring hope. He specifically named the regions of Zebulun and Naphtali in Galilee, towns on the northern edge of Israel. After generations of war with Assyria and Babylon, many of those foreigners settled among the Israelites, bringing their pagan beliefs and practices with them. Over time, the people living there drifted away from the God who loved them. That is why Isaiah prophesied, "In the past he humbled the land of Zebulun and the land of Naphtali, but in the future, he will honor Galilee … The people walking in darkness have seen a great light" (Isaiah 9:1–2).

Jesus was the fulfillment of that prophecy. He was, and is, that light.

Jesus Heals and Hope Spreads

Word about the countless miracles Jesus performed spread all over the region. He healed Peter's mother-in-law when she was sick (Luke 4:38–39). He helped a lame man walk again (Luke 5:24–25). Before long, his name and works were known throughout Galilee; the crowds came to Him, desperate for help and hungry for truth (Matthew 4:23–25).

The Sermon on the Mount

One day, a large crowd gathered around Jesus to hear Him speak, so He walked up a hillside and sat down with His disciples nearby (Matthew 5:1). The people came closer and leaned forward so they wouldn't miss a word. Then Jesus explained to them who was truly blessed; it wasn't the strong or wealthy, but the humble and kind. He continued:

"Blessed are the poor in spirit, for theirs is the kingdom of heaven.

Blessed are those who mourn, for they will be comforted.

Blessed are the meek, for they will inherit the earth.

Blessed are those who hunger and thirst for righteousness, for they will be filled.

Blessed are the merciful, for they will be shown mercy.

Blessed are the pure in heart, for they will see God.

Blessed are the peacemakers, for they will be called children of God.

Blessed are those who are persecuted because of righteousness, for theirs is the kingdom of heaven" (Matthew 5:3–10).

After teaching about the blessing, Jesus looked out into the crowd and said, "You are the salt of the earth" (Matthew 5:13). Just as salt brings out the best flavor in food, followers of God are meant to bring out the goodness of God in the world around them. Jesus wanted His people to live out their faith every day by helping others through kindness, truth, and love. He commanded them not only to love their neighbors and friends, but also to love their enemies. "But I tell you, love your enemies and pray for those who persecute you," He said (Matthew 5:44).

He also reminded them to "Do to others what you would have them do to you" (Matthew 7:12). This is the Golden Rule. It was important not just to hear God's word but to live it out daily. Jesus explained this could be achieved by forgiving instead of seeking revenge, accepting others instead of judging, and helping others with our resources instead of holding them back for ourselves.

To reiterate the importance of following His words, Jesus finished the day with a story everyone could understand. He shared that a person who hears His words and lives by them daily is like a wise person who has built their house on solid ground. When a heavy thunderstorm blows in, that house stands strong. But the person who listens to His words and does nothing with them is like a foolish person who has built their house on sand. When the storm comes, the house collapses with a great fall (Matthew 7:24–27).

The people were amazed to hear this truth and knew Jesus spoke with authority (Matthew 7:28–29).

Why This Story Matters

Jesus' message was one of hope and an invitation to a better life. He wasn't sent to erase the old laws of the Bible; He came to fulfill them. He added that true change is about more than how we act on the outside. Jesus cares about our inward transformation, our motives, and the obedience of our hearts.

He revealed the clear contrast between the Kingdom of God and the ways of this world. While the world elevates power, pride, status, and self-promotion, Jesus called us to a different way of living, one that notices the forgotten, comforts the hurting, practices gratitude, patience, and mercy, and pursues a genuine relationship with God our Father.

The Sermon on the Mount explained what it truly means to follow Jesus, to live under God's reign, and to reflect the values of His Kingdom, not only by our faith but also by our actions. Jesus called His followers, then and now, to a faith that shapes our character, our choices, and the way we treat others. When we live this way, people don't just hear the message of the Kingdom, they see it.

A Prayer to End

Jesus' disciples asked Him to teach them how to pray to God. He gave them a simple prayer that reminded them to trust God, forgive others, and do what is right and good. He shared what is known today as the Lord's prayer:

"Our Father in heaven, hallowed be your name, your kingdom come, your will be done, on earth as it is in heaven. Give us today our daily bread. And forgive us our debts, as we also have forgiven our debtors. And lead us not into temptation, but deliver us from the evil one" (Matthew 6:9–13). For thine is the Kingdom and the power, and the glory, now and forever. Amen.

Bible References

Matthew 14 — John the Baptist put in prison
Matthew 4 — Jesus begins His ministry
Isaiah 9 — Prophecy of light in Galilee
Luke 4 — Jesus heals Simon's mother-in-law
Luke 5 — A lame man walks
Matthew 5–7 — Sermon on the Mount
Matthew 6 — The Lord's Prayer

Pause & Reflect — Surrender

Lay Your Burdens at His Feet

None of us was ever meant to carry the everyday burdens and anxieties of life on our own. In Scripture, the weight a person carries is often described as a yoke. A yoke is a wooden beam placed across the neck of an animal, attached to a plow, used to pull heavy loads through hard ground. It was designed for strength and endurance, not ease. When Jesus speaks of taking our yoke or offering us His, He is speaking directly to the weight of worry, regret, fear, and pressure we carry each day.

Jesus does not deny that life is difficult. He knows the brokenness that entered the world after the fall, and He understands the struggles we face because of sin, pain, and loss. But God, in His mercy, sent Jesus so we would not have to walk through life alone. Jesus invites us to bring our burdens to Him, not because we are weak, but because He is strong. He reminds us, "Take my yoke upon you and learn from me, for I am gentle and humble in heart, and you will find rest for your souls. For my yoke is easy and my burden is light" (Matthew 11:29–30).

Satan often tells us we should be ashamed of our struggles, that we should be able to push through, figure things out, and carry it all ourselves. But Jesus says the opposite. When we come to Him in prayer and lay our worries at His feet, we are renewed. We begin to live the life God intended, not weighed down by fear or regret, but strengthened by trust. Humbling ourselves before Jesus and releasing what we carry is not a weakness. It is an act of faith.

Memory Verse

"Come to me, all you who are weary and burdened, and I will give you rest." — Matthew 11:28

Questions to Consider

What burdens are we still trying to carry alone?

Where have we been resisting Jesus' rest?

A Prayer to End

Dear Jesus, thank You for inviting us to bring our burdens to You. Help us release the worries, regrets, and fears we were never meant to carry. Teach us to trust You fully and to rest in Your strength instead of relying on our own. Give us the courage to lay everything at Your feet and to believe Your way truly leads to peace. Amen.

READING 15

In the Year of Our Lord, ~AD 31

The Centurion's Faith; Compassion for the Widow

The Roman Who Believed

There was a Roman centurion who lived in the fishing village of Capernaum. He was a high-ranking officer in the Roman army who had authority over one hundred soldiers. Centurions were responsible for their men and for handling the flow of supplies that came through their areas of responsibility. So, to many people living in the town, centurions seemed fearless and strong. But behind this centurion's armor was a heart of gold.

He was a Gentile, a non-Jew, who served in the Roman army that ruled over Israel. Usually, Gentiles did not observe Jewish religious traditions, but this man was genuinely interested in Jewish customs and their faith; he was especially curious about the God they prayed to. He noticed Jews worshiped differently than the Romans he grew up with. Something convinced him that the God the Jews believed in was real.

The centurion wanted to learn more about their God, but as a Gentile, he wasn't allowed to go into a synagogue or be taught by a rabbi (Acts 10:28). Still, he stayed true to his heart. He gave generously to those in need and helped the Jewish community build their synagogue with his own money (Luke 7:5). At that time, a Roman citizen supporting another people's God could be dangerous if other Roman officials found out. They might have questioned his loyalty to Caesar, the Roman emperor. But the centurion wasn't worried. He could not deny his heart was drawn to the God of Israel.

One day, the centurion learned his most trusted servant suffered from an untreatable illness (Luke 7:2). Saddened by this news, he desperately sought help for his friend.

The centurion had heard of Jesus, the rabbi and healer who performed miracles, healed many people, and spoke with authority. Naturally, he thought Jesus might be the answer to his prayers, but he felt unworthy to meet with Him face-to-face. So the centurion asked some of the local Jewish elders to speak to Jesus on his behalf (Luke 7:3).

They agreed, and when they found Jesus, they said, "This man deserves to have you do this, because he loves our nation and has built our synagogue" (Luke 7:4–5). So, Jesus went back with them.

As they made their way to his house, the centurion sent another group to meet Jesus with this message: "Lord, don't trouble yourself, for I do not deserve to have you come under my roof. That is why I did not even consider myself worthy to come to you. But say the word, and my servant will be healed" (Luke 7:6–7). Jesus stopped, looked around at those with Him, and said, "I tell you, I have not found such great faith even in Israel" (Luke 7:9).

By the time the messengers arrived at the centurion's house, they found the servant already up and completely healed (Luke 7:10).

Jesus Shows Compassion for a Widow's Loss

Not long after, Jesus traveled thirty miles to the town of Nain with His disciples and a large crowd of followers. As they approached the town entrance, a funeral procession came out of the city gate (Luke 7:11–12). A young man had passed away, and people carried his body in an open casket. A woman walked slowly in step with the procession, crying so hard she could barely stand.

The tearful woman was the boy's mother. She had recently lost her husband, and now, her only son was gone too. In those days, a woman without a husband or a son to provide for her struggled to survive. She had lost everyone and was now on her own.

Yet, Jesus saw her. Not the anguish on her face but the pain in her heart. He felt sorry for her and said in a gentle voice, "Don't cry" (Luke 7:13). He then walked up to the casket, touched it, and said, "Young man, I say to you, get up!" (Luke 7:14).

To everyone's astonishment, the young man sat up full of life (Luke 7:15). The crowd stood in awe, and news of Jesus' power and compassion spread far and wide (Luke 7:16–17).

Why This Story Matters

These two stories show us that Jesus responds not only to our voices but also to our hearts.

The centurion was an outsider who quietly supported the Jewish people, helping them build their synagogue. This defiant act, if made public, could have been seen as an act of treason against the Roman Empire. But he didn't care; his heart yearned for the God of Israel. Though he felt unworthy to approach Jesus face-to-face, his humble faith spoke volumes, and Jesus honored "such great faith."

The widow in Nain grieved the death of her only son, yet didn't say a word. She was heartbroken, her future uncertain, and her livelihood in jeopardy. She didn't ask Jesus for a single thing, but He saw her fear, loneliness, and her silent cry for help. And He stepped in with compassion.

These moments remind us that faith doesn't have to be loud, just genuine. Jesus sees those who actively seek Him, as well as those who are barely hanging on. He answers the hearts that long for Him, even when we can't get the words out.

A Prayer to End

Dear Jesus, thank You for being the kind of Savior who sees what others overlook. You notice the faith that is quiet, the hearts that are searching, and the pain words can't express. Help us trust You even when we feel unworthy. Like the centurion, may we believe in Your power, even from a distance. And like the widow, when we are too overwhelmed to speak, remind us You still hear the cries of our hearts. Amen.

Bible References

Acts 10 — Gentiles and the Jewish faith
Luke 7 — Jesus heals the centurion's servant and raises the widow's son

In the Year of Our Lord, ~AD 31

The Parable of the Sower; Calming the Storm

Teaching by the Sea

The Sea of Galilee glistened in the afternoon sun as large crowds gathered along its shoreline. People from all walks of life came from towns near and far, eager to hear Jesus speak (Mark 4:1). He used simple stories, known as parables, with powerful meanings to get His message across. Those in attendance leaned in as Jesus spoke.

The Parable of the Sower

"A farmer went out to sow his seed. As he was scattering the seed, some fell along the path, and the birds came and ate it up. Some fell on rocky places, where it did not have much soil. It sprang up quickly because the soil was shallow. But when the sun came up, the plants were scorched, and they withered because they had no root. Other seed fell among thorns, which grew up and choked the plants, so that they did not bear grain. Still other seed fell on good soil. It came up, grew, and produced a crop, some multiplying thirty, some sixty, some a hundred times" (Mark 4:3–8).

Once the crowds left and Jesus was alone with His disciples, they asked Him what the parable meant (Mark 4:10). Jesus shared, "The seed is the word of God. Those along the path are the ones who hear, and then the devil comes and takes away the word from their hearts, so that they may not believe and be saved (Luke 8:11–12).

"Those on the rocky ground are the ones who receive the word with joy when they hear it, but they have no root. They believe for a while, but in the time of testing, they fall away" (Luke 8:13). These are people whose hearts have been hardened. Life has made them skeptical, not trusting, or callous. When storms of life come their way, they rely on their own strength and understanding rather than the truth they once accepted.

Jesus continued, "The seed that fell among thorns stands for those who hear, but as they go on their way they are choked by life's worries, riches and pleasures, and they do not mature (Luke 8:14). Their hearts are not hardened like the rocky soil, but they are conflicted and eventually stop growing in faith. God's word gets lost, competing with earthly distractions. They may have once trusted and believed in God, but now their eyes have shifted toward worldly pursuits.

Then Jesus ended the parable by saying, "But the seed on good soil stands for those with a noble and good heart, who hear the word, retain it, and by persevering [through both the good times and bad] produce a crop" (Luke 8:15). These are hearts open to God, strong and humble, where His word takes root and grows strong.

The disciples listened carefully, still thinking about the meaning of what they had just heard. Then Jesus said to them, "Let us go over to the other side [of the lake]" (Mark 4:35).

Jesus Calms the Storm

His disciples set sail across the Sea of Galilee while Jesus lay down in the boat to rest (Mark 4:36, 38). At first, the lake was calm, but suddenly, the skies darkened, strong winds gushed in, and waves crashed over the sides of the boat. The disciples, who had faced many storms before, tried to steady the vessel but could not. They were terrified.

In a panic, they woke Jesus up and yelled, "Teacher, don't you care if we drown?" (Mark 4:38). Jesus stood up, looked at the crashing waves, and said, "Quiet! Be still!" Immediately, the howling wind stopped. The waves calmed down, and the sea was peaceful once again (Mark 4:39). Then Jesus turned toward His disciples and asked them, "Why are you so afraid? Do you still have no faith?" (Mark 4:40).

The disciples stood there in awe, whispering to each other, "Who is this? Even the wind and waves obey Him!" (Mark 4:41).

Why This Story Matters

Sometimes we hear God's word, and it sounds great, full of hope, truth, and love. But then life happens, and we get busy, stressed out, and worried. Just like the seed that landed on rocky ground or was choked by thorns, our hearts can also become hard, distracted, and tired.

Then there are times like the disciples experienced in the boat. When storms of life come our way, we often stress out over things we cannot control, forgetting He is always with us. We tend to rely on our own strength, trying to muscle our way through the storm to keep our boat from sinking.

But Jesus invites us to trust Him, to rely on Him to help keep our heads above water.

The same loving, merciful God who plants His word into our hearts is the same One who calms the storms in our lives. He knows all about the strength of the waves and the heights of our failures, yet He asks us to believe in Him — not just when it's easy, but especially when it's hard.

A Prayer to End

Dear God, thank You for giving us Your word and for planting truth into our hearts. Keep our hearts from becoming filled with life's worries, so they remain open and ready to receive what You want to teach us. When storms come our way, help us not to panic or rely on ourselves, but to remember You are with us. You are stronger than any wave, and more faithful than our fears. Amen.

Bible References

Mark 4 — Parable of the sower; Jesus calms the storm
Luke 8 — Meaning of the parable explained

In the Year of Our Lord, ~AD 31

The Story of Two Lives Restored

Living Among the Tombs

After calming the storm on the Sea of Galilee, Jesus and His disciples decided to continue to sail across the water. The sea was much quieter now, but the disciples were still full of questions and wonder after witnessing Jesus speak with authority over the weather.

Later that afternoon, they finally reached the other side of the lake, a distant region called the Gerasenes (Mark 5:1). It was a land occupied by Gentiles, a non-Jewish people, so most Israelites never traveled there. But Jesus did; He had a purpose.

The boat reached the shore near a series of tombs. These tombs were caves carved into rock, often owned by families and used as burial places for the dead. Before Jesus and His disciples got out of the boat, a man came running out of the tombs (Mark 5:2). His eyes were wild, and his hair was completely tangled. Chains, broken and rusted, hung off his arms and legs. People in the nearby town feared him and believed he was demon-possessed. He had lived alone among the tombs for a very long time. The townspeople had tried to chain him up, but he broke free every time. No one could help him. Every day, he cried out, hurting himself and scaring people. But he didn't scare Jesus (Mark 5:3–5).

The man collapsed at Jesus' feet and shouted, "What do you want with me, Jesus, Son of the Most High God?" (Mark 5:7). Jesus saw that the man was in pain; he was trapped by an evil spirit. "Come out of this man, you impure spirit!" Jesus commanded (Mark 5:8).

Before coming out of him, the demons inside the man begged Jesus to send them to a nearby herd of pigs. He allowed it, and at once, the unclean spirits left the man and entered the pigs. The entire herd ran down the hillside and continued into the lake and drowned (Mark 5:11–13).

The townspeople came running when they heard the news. They found the man sitting calmly at Jesus' feet, dressed and now in his right mind. He was finally free! The people were amazed but also confused about what had just happened. Out of fear, they asked Jesus to leave (Mark 5:14–17).

As Jesus prepared to board the boat and leave, the healed man pleaded to go with Him. But Jesus said, "Go home to your own people and tell them how much the Lord has done for you, and how he has had mercy on you." So, the man left, telling everyone what Jesus had done (Mark 5:18–20).

An Unlikely Request from a Respected Leader

Jesus and His disciples sailed back across the lake to the town of Capernaum (Mark 5:21). When they arrived, a large crowd waited for them on the shoreline.

One man, eager to see Jesus, pushed through the crowd. His name was Jairus, a respected synagogue leader. Even though he was an important man, Jairus dropped to his knees in front of Jesus and begged Him, "My little daughter is dying. Please come and put your hands on her so that she will be healed and live" (Mark 5:22–23).

Jesus agreed, and He, Jairus, and the crowd started walking toward Jairus' home. Along the way, they were greeted by a messenger from Jairus' house. "Your daughter is dead," he said quietly. "Why bother the teacher anymore?" (Mark 5:35). Jairus was devastated. But Jesus said to him, "Don't be afraid; just believe" (Mark 5:36).

A Young Girl Awakens

When they reached Jairus' house, the people were weeping and mourning. Jesus questioned them, "Why all this commotion and wailing? The child is not dead but asleep." At this, they all laughed at Him (Mark 5:38–40).

Jesus went inside the home along with the girl's father and mother, and three of His disciples, Peter, James, and John. They all went upstairs into the room where the child lay. Then, Jesus gently took the girl's hand and said, "Talitha koum!" which means, "Little girl, I say to you, get up!" Immediately, the twelve-year-old girl opened her eyes, took a deep breath, and stood up. Her parents were overwhelmed and marveled at what had just taken place (Mark 5:40–42).

Jesus then asked her parents to feed her and not to tell anyone what happened (Mark 5:43).

Why This Story Matters

Jesus crossed a stormy sea for one man, a man who had been pushed out of his community and forgotten. Those living nearby saw someone unworthy, dangerous, and beyond hope, someone who deserved to be locked away in chains instead of receiving compassion. But Jesus saw value in one man, a person who still had purpose in God's story, because every life matters to Him.

Then there was Jairus, a well-respected synagogue leader, who likely had dismissed Jesus previously. But when his daughter was dying, he became desperate and bowed at the feet of the very One he once doubted. Jairus came in fear, surrounded by voices that mocked Jesus. Yet Jesus simply reached out and healed the little girl; He knew it was the right, good, and merciful thing to do.

Jesus is near to every kind of person: the forgotten, the skeptical, the desperate, and the new believer. True peace, hope, and restoration come only through the One sent for us. All who come to Him in faith are welcomed by the King of kings, the One who still heals, still guides, and still gives new life.

A Prayer to End

Dear Jesus, thank You for crossing through the storms, the wind, and the rain to reach even one life in need of Your salvation. Thank You for seeing value in every person, especially those who feel hopeless, lost, or forgotten. Give us the strength to keep going in a world that often pushes against Your ways. And when we stumble or doubt along the way, like Jairus once did, give us the courage to return to You again. Amen.

Bible References

Mark 5 — The demon-possessed man and Jairus' daughter

In the Year of Our Lord, ~AD 31

Jesus Instructs His Disciples — Go Out!

The Journey Begins

Jesus went from town to town, teaching with His twelve disciples. The crowds around them continued to grow. The needs of those in the region were great, and the message Jesus shared gave hope and peace to all who came to hear the truth. But His message needed to be shared beyond just one town or region. So, Jesus gave His disciples a new mission: to go out and preach and heal the people wherever the disciples were accepted (Mark 6:6–7).

And then He added a directive that surprised everyone: "Take nothing for the journey except a staff," He said. "No bread, no bag, no money in your belts. Wear sandals but not an extra shirt" (Mark 6:8–9).

The disciples looked at each other, unsure if Jesus was serious. Nothing? No extra clothes or supplies? No food for the journey?

Jesus continued, "Whenever you enter a house, stay there until you leave that town. And if any place will not welcome you or listen to you, leave that place and shake the dust off your feet as a testimony against them" (Mark 6:10–11). So, they left, nervous about their journey but trusting in Him.

What happened as they went on their way was wonderful.

In town after town, the disciples taught the people about God's Kingdom. They cast out evil spirits and anointed the sick with oil and saw many people healed (Mark 6:12–13). Many in the crowd also turned their hearts back to God after hearing the Good News, the message of salvation found only through belief in Jesus Christ.

A Joyful Return

The disciples returned after several days of traveling. Their eyes were wide with excitement. Their voices spilled over one another as they eagerly told Jesus all that had happened. But soon, their joy was mixed with exhaustion as the crowds gathered around them again, still asking for help, healing, and truth.

Jesus looked at them kindly and said, "Come with me by yourselves to a quiet place and get some rest" (Mark 6:31). They got back in the boat and sailed across the Sea of Galilee, hoping to find a peaceful spot.

Jesus Feeds Five Thousand

But the quiet rest they were seeking never came. The villagers saw them leaving by boat and hurried along the shore after them. By the time Jesus and the disciples arrived on the other side, more than five thousand people were already gathered there waiting for them. The disciples might have groaned inside upon seeing the crowd, but Jesus didn't. Instead, He looked at the people and felt deep compassion for them because they were like sheep without a shepherd (Mark 6:33–34). Even though Jesus was tired, He taught them throughout the day.

As the day came to an end, the disciples said, "This is a remote place, and it's already very late. Send the people away so that they can go to the surrounding countryside and villages and buy themselves something to eat." But Jesus replied, "You give them something to eat." They were confused. "That would take more than half a year's wages!" someone said. Jesus asked, "How many loaves do you have?" After searching, they returned with five loaves of bread and two fish (Mark 6:35–38).

Jesus had the people sit down in groups on the grass. He took the loaves and fish, looked up to heaven, and gave thanks. Then He broke the bread and gave it to His disciples to distribute (Mark 6:39–41). As they passed the food around, something miraculous happened: the food never ran out! Everyone ate until they were full. When supper was over, the disciples collected twelve basketfuls of leftovers (Mark 6:42–44).

Why This Story Matters

Jesus knew the time of His death was drawing near. A big part of His mission was to ensure His disciples were prepared to continue His ministry after He returned to heaven. So, He sent them out, not to test their readiness, but to build their confidence and trust in God.

When they returned, celebrating their success and works done through the Father, it looked like they might be ready. But when challenged with how to feed five thousand people, their faith faltered. They forgot what God could do through them. Yet Jesus did not get upset or give up on them. Instead, He showed them once again that with true faith in God, nothing is impossible.

Perfect faith does not happen overnight. These stories remind us that our faith journey will have moments of courage and moments of weakness. But Jesus is patient in every moment, and when we call on Him, He gives us the strength and wisdom to do great things in His holy name.

A Prayer to End

Dear Jesus, thank You for sending us, even when we do not feel perfectly prepared. Thank You for reminding us that when we walk by faith, You always provide everything we need. Help us trust You like the disciples did when they went out with nothing. Teach us to give what we have, even when it feels small, and trust You to bless it. And when we falter, lift us back up. Amen.

Bible References

Mark 6 — Jesus sends out the Twelve and feeds the five thousand

In the Year of Our Lord, ~AD 31

Jesus Walks on Water

The Disciples Cross the Sea

After an incredible day of listening to Jesus teach and being fed from five loaves and two fish, many in the crowd lingered near the shore and spent time getting to know one another. While the people shared stories and talked about the day's events, Jesus gently dismissed them for the day. Then, He turned to His disciples and told them to get back in the boat and cross the lake, and assured them He would join them later.

The disciples were still buzzing with excitement over everything that had just happened, but they obeyed Jesus, got into their boat, and began rowing across the Sea of Galilee.

Jesus Prays Alone

Understandably, Jesus was exhausted from a full day of teaching and healing the masses, so He decided to go somewhere quiet to pray and spend time with His Father (Matthew 14:23). The quietness Jesus experienced on the mountaintop was a sharp contrast to the noise of the crowd He had just left. There, in the still of the night, He prayed while He watched over His disciples from a distance. Jesus often withdrew like this and found strength through prayer and reflection. In these quiet moments, He prepared His heart for what was ahead.

Hours later, now well past midnight, the disciples were far from shore, and the weather around them got worse. Strong winds picked up, and waves crashed over their boat. No matter how hard they rowed, they made very little progress (Mark 6:47–48). As fatigue set in, their joy from earlier in the day quickly faded into worry.

As the disciples struggled to control their boat, they had no idea something unbelievable was about to happen (Matthew 14:25).

The Collision of Faith and Fear

During the height of the storm, between three and six in the morning, the wind howled, and waves slapped the sides of the boat. Suddenly, the disciples saw the shadow of a figure moving toward them on the water … not around the water, but walking on top of it! They were terrified. "It's a ghost," they cried out, their fear rocking them to the core (Matthew

14:26). But then a familiar voice called out above the wind, a voice that was calm and strong: "Take courage! It is I. Don't be afraid" (Matthew 14:27).

Peter, always the confident one, called back, "Lord, if it's you, tell me to come to you on the water." Jesus said, "Come" (Matthew 14:28–29). So, Peter bravely stepped out of the boat and into the open water, and for a moment, he too walked on water. With his eyes locked on Jesus, he did what no one else in the boat dared to try. Then the storm intensified; the wind blew harder. Distracted, Peter looked away from Jesus. As his focus turned to the storm around him, fear overtook him, and just like that, he began to sink (Matthew 14:30).

"Lord, save me!" Peter cried.

Immediately, Jesus reached out His hand and took hold of him. "You of little faith," He said, "why did you doubt?" (Matthew 14:31).

An Immature Faith

When they climbed back into the boat, the wind suddenly stopped, and the sea grew calm again (Matthew 14:32). The disciples looked at each other in pure amazement. They worshiped Jesus and said, "Truly you are the Son of God" (Matthew 14:33).

Why This Story Matters

This was the second time in a row the disciples had the opportunity to exercise their belief, and they hesitated. Just the day before, Jesus told them to feed a crowd of five thousand, and they insisted it couldn't be done. But it happened. Now, in the middle of a midnight storm, they were overwhelmed once again.

They forgot how Jesus had calmed another storm with a single word. They forgot how faith had already helped them when Jesus sent them out to teach and heal. And they forgot what they were capable of when they moved in the power and authority of Jesus Christ.

But Jesus didn't perform miracles to impress His disciples. He was training them, preparing their hearts for what was coming after He was gone. He knew they would face storms, not only on the water, but in real life. He wanted them to grasp something essential: When we fix our eyes on Him, we can walk through any storm. But when we take our eyes off Jesus and try to go it alone, we begin to sink.

A Prayer to End

Dear Jesus, thank You for sharing the story of Peter and the disciples in the storm. It reminds us that even those closest to You didn't always recognize You right away. Forgive us for the times we doubt or lose sight of who You are. When we face life's storms, help us keep our focus on You and not on the troubles around us. Teach us through the stories in Your word that ordinary people with extraordinary faith can do amazing things. Amen.

Bible References

Matthew 14 — Jesus walks on water
Mark 6 — Jesus walks on the lake and calms the storm

READING 20

In the Year of Our Lord, ~AD 31

The Story of the Good Samaritan

Question About Eternal Life

As Jesus made His way through the towns and villages of Judea, the people followed Him wherever He went. Some in the crowd were genuinely interested in what Jesus had to say and leaned forward, soaking up every word, while others stood in the back with their arms crossed, skeptical, hoping to catch Him sharing untruths. But, despite the different motives, it didn't stop one man from coming forward and asking a question that led Jesus to share one of His most unforgettable stories (Luke 10:25).

This man had studied the law of God his entire life, and he stood up to test Jesus with a serious question: "Teacher, what must I do to inherit eternal life?" Jesus turned the question back to him. "What is written in the Law?" He asked. The man answered, "Love the Lord your God with all your heart and with all your soul and with all your strength and with all your mind; and love your neighbor as yourself." Jesus nodded. "You have answered correctly. Do this and you will live" (Luke 10:26–28).

The man wanted to appear wise, so he asked Jesus, "And who is my neighbor?" (Luke 10:29).

To answer that question, Jesus told a story that took everyone listening by surprise.

The Good Samaritan

One day, a Jewish man traveled on foot from Jerusalem to Jericho, two towns that were seventeen miles apart. The way was steep, and the road was dangerous, known for its twists and turns and hiding places where robbers waited for unsuspecting travelers. As the man walked by, a group of thieves jumped out and attacked him, taking everything he had and leaving him badly injured. He lay on the ground, bleeding, bruised, and barely alive.

A couple of hours later, a priest walked by and saw the wounded man lying by the side of the road. But instead of helping, he crossed to the other side of the road and continued on his journey.

Next came a Levite, someone who also worked in the temple and taught others about God. He, like the priest, saw the man lying there but walked by without stopping; he acted like he hadn't seen anything.

Finally, a Samaritan came walking up the road (Luke 10:30–33).

The people listening to Jesus knew Jews from the Southern Kingdom and Samaritans from the Northern Kingdom did not get along. For hundreds of years, these two people groups had argued about religion, worship traditions, and temple locations. Most Jews saw Samaritans as outsiders who had mixed Gentile beliefs. So, Jesus mentioning a Samaritan in His story probably captured everyone's attention even more.

Unlike the priest and the Levite, this Samaritan didn't walk by. He saw the man, felt compassion for him, and helped him. Gently, the Samaritan cleaned up the man's wounds with water and oil and covered them with a soft cloth. Then he put the man on his own donkey and took him to an inn.

That night, he took care of him. And the next day he gave the innkeeper money and said, "Look after him, and when I return, I will reimburse you for any extra expense you may have" (Luke 10:34–35).

The Conversation That Came After

When Jesus finished telling the story, He asked the man who had probed about who qualifies as a neighbor, "Which of these three do you think was a neighbor to the man who fell into the hands of robbers?"

The man replied, "The one who had mercy on him."

Jesus said, "Go and do likewise" (Luke 10:36–37).

Why This Story Matters

This story isn't just about being kind; it's about being courageous. Jesus wanted His listeners to understand what real love looked like in action. The man who was attacked while traveling was most likely a southern Jew. The first two men who walked past him, a priest and a Levite, were also southern Jews, people who were expected to help — but they didn't. They walked right past their own neighbor.

But not the Samaritan.

When he saw the injured traveler by the side of the road, his heart broke. He didn't see an enemy; he saw a person alone, in pain, and left to die. In that moment, he decided to love deeply, personally, and sacrificially. That's what Jesus means by "love your neighbor." Not just when it's easy, not just when the person agrees with or looks like us, but when it's uncomfortable, inconvenient, and costly.

The Samaritan showed mercy by stopping to help the man he didn't know, while others walked on by. He showed grace by going beyond what was expected, tending to the man's wounds, placing him on his own animal, and paying for his care at the inn. The Samaritan did more than was expected and didn't expect anything in return.

When our hearts are transformed, we are able to love with compassion, no longer allowing differences to stop us from helping our neighbor. This kind of love does not look for applause or recognition. It loves quietly, even when no one is watching, because it reflects the heart of Jesus. As we love this way, we grow into the people God wants us to be.

A Prayer to End

Dear Jesus, thank You for showing us what being a good neighbor really looks like. It means loving beyond boundaries, forgiving across divides, and choosing compassion over indifference. May our hearts break for what breaks Yours. Help us be more like the Good Samaritan, giving sacrificially and expecting nothing in return. When someone is in pain, give us the courage to move toward them and lend a hand, instead of backing away and pretending we don't see what's right in front of us. Amen.

Bible References

Luke 10 — Jesus teaches who a true neighbor is

Pause & Reflect — Discipleship

Help Us Seek You Daily

Jesus taught His disciples, and those who followed Him, that knowing Him required more than belief alone. To grow in faith, they would need to live differently. Discipleship was never about checking boxes or following rules out of obligation. It was about consistency, choosing each day to walk closely with Him through prayer, obedience, and time in God's Word.

When we build our lives on Jesus' truth and allow our roots to grow deep, we are anchored to a solid foundation. This kind of faith allows us to withstand the storms of life, not by our own strength, but by His. Being grounded in His truth also helps us stand firm against the constant pressure to conform to the patterns and values of the world around us.

As we seek Jesus daily and remain in His Word, our lives begin to reflect His heart. Scripture reminds us, "Your word is a lamp for my feet, a light on my path" (Psalm 119:105). Discipleship shapes who we are becoming, guiding our steps and allowing others to see Jesus through the way we love, serve, and live.

Memory Verse

"If you hold to my teaching, you are really my disciples. Then you will know the truth, and the truth will set you free." — John 8:31–32

Questions to Consider

What simple step can we take to spend more consistent time in God's word?

How can we approach prayer in a way that feels more honest and personal, rather than routine?

A Prayer to End

Dear Jesus, thank You for inviting us into a daily relationship with You. Help us seek You with intention, not out of obligation, but out of love and trust. Teach us to remain rooted in Your truth and to build our lives on the solid foundation You provide. Shape our hearts, guide our steps, and help our lives reflect You in all we say and do. Amen.

In the Year of Our Lord, ~AD 32

Jesus Predicts His Death and Resurrection

False Worship to False Gods

Jesus and His disciples traveled from village to village, teaching the people about God's Kingdom and filling them with hope. During their time together, the disciples witnessed Jesus healing the sick, casting out demons, and even calming the seas. The crowds marveled at His miracles, but many still didn't understand who this man from Nazareth truly was.

One day, Jesus and His disciples traveled to the north, far beyond the familiar towns near the Sea of Galilee. They arrived in a town called Caesarea Philippi, tucked into the base of Mount Hermon. This village was unlike any other they had visited before. Caesarea Philippi was known across the region for worshiping false idols, and the people there had built a temple dedicated to the Greek god Pan, a half-man, half-goat creature that lived in the woods and played a pan flute. The town was filled with statues, temples, and symbols of Roman authority and pagan religion.

It was there, in the presence of man-made gods and worldly power, that Jesus asked His disciples a simple but important question.

"Who do people say the Son of Man is?" He asked as they walked together (Matthew 16:13).

They took turns answering Jesus, "Some say John the Baptist; others say [the Prophet] Elijah; and still others, Jeremiah or one of the prophets." Then Jesus looked at each of them and asked a more revealing question than the first: "But what about you? Who do you say I am?" (Matthew 16:14–15).

They fell silent. Then Peter, confident, bold, and faithful, spoke up. "You are the Messiah," he said, "the Son of the living God" (Matthew 16:16).

His response marked a big turning point for the disciples. In the middle of a town filled with false gods, Peter declared that Jesus was the One, the living Messiah, sent by God. His answer pleased Jesus. He told Peter that God must have revealed this truth to him, not human knowledge, but divine, inspired wisdom. Jesus said, "You are Peter, and on this rock I will build my church, and the gates of Hades will not overcome it" (Matthew 16:17–18).

Jesus Describes His Road to the Cross

But soon after that joyful moment, Jesus began to explain coming events that were difficult for the disciples to hear. He told them He would leave for Jerusalem soon, suffer greatly, be rejected by the elders and teachers of the law, be killed, and after three days, rise again (Mark 8:31).

Peter couldn't believe what he heard. This wasn't the victorious ending he had imagined for his King. He quickly approached Jesus, pulled Him aside, and began to rebuke Him. In other words, Peter tried to change Jesus' mind. He shouted sternly, "Never, Lord! This will never happen to you!" (Matthew 16:22).

But Jesus cut Peter off and gave him a rebuke of His own. He said, "Get behind me, Satan! You are a stumbling block to me; you do not have in mind the concerns of God, but merely human concerns" (Matthew 16:23).

Jesus wasn't saying Peter was the devil, but He recognized Peter's words echoed the same temptation Satan had presented earlier in the wilderness. Peter was unknowingly offering an easier path, one without suffering or the cross. Jesus knew that even words spoken out of care could distract Him from God's plan.

Jesus remained faithful and obedient to His Father's will, even knowing it would lead to pain and death. Peter, however, could not yet see or understand God's greater purpose, that Jesus had to suffer and die to save the world. Nothing, not even the concern of a close friend, could turn Jesus away from completing the mission He had been sent to fulfill.

Why This Story Matters

This story shows us the deep commitment Jesus had in carrying out His Father's plan. Even when Peter, His close friend, tried to show Him a way out, Jesus stayed the course. Jesus knew the stakes; His mission was eternal. He knew our salvation would only come through His suffering and death, just as it was written in the Old Testament by prophets like Isaiah who described the future Messiah this way: "He was despised and rejected by mankind, a man of suffering, and familiar with pain" (Isaiah 53:3).

Even though Peter had openly announced Jesus as the Messiah, he and the other disciples didn't fully understand these prophecies yet. They had grown up hearing some of the Scriptures but hadn't grasped the fact that Jesus would have to suffer. Jesus' strong response to Peter reminds us that God's plans are usually bigger and more difficult than we expect, but they are always right.

We also see how Jesus and His disciples traveled to Caesarea Philippi. They entered a place known for idol worship, spiritual darkness, and danger. It was a region many people of faith avoided, yet Jesus went there on purpose. He brought healing, hope, and truth into a place that desperately needed it.

Today, we are called to do the same. Our mission is not only to share the Gospel within our comfort zones, but to bring the love of Jesus to those the world overlooks. It is in those very places that God's Kingdom advances, restoring hearts and changing lives.

A Prayer to End

Dear God, thank You for showing us that true faith sometimes means walking a difficult path but having the courage to stay the course with You by our side. Thank You for giving Jesus the strength and courage to face the cross on our behalf when He could have run from it. Help us trust Your plans completely, even when we don't fully understand them yet. Give us hearts like Peter's, ready to believe, but also hearts that are open to correction when we need help. Amen.

Bible References

Matthew 16 — Peter declares Jesus is the Messiah
Mark 8 — Jesus predicts His death and resurrection
Isaiah 53 — The suffering Messiah is foretold

Where Judgment Ends and Grace Begins

The Woman Caught in Adultery

Throughout Jesus' ministry, He taught His disciples not only with words, but through the way He lived. Every step He took and every interaction He had revealed the heart of God. He called His followers to love their neighbors, pray for their enemies, and allow their hearts to be transformed so others might come to know God personally through Him.

In one unforgettable moment, religious leaders brought a woman caught in adultery before Jesus (John 8:3). Their goal was not restoration, but entrapment. They hoped to force Jesus into a statement they could use against Him. The crowd gathered quickly, forming a circle around the woman, stones already in hand. According to the law they followed, her punishment was death (John 8:5).

They asked Jesus what should be done.

Instead of responding with anger or debate, Jesus bent down and wrote on the ground (John 8:6). Then He stood and spoke words that forever changed the atmosphere. "Let any one of you who is without sin be the first to throw a stone" (John 8:7).

Silence followed.

One by one, the stones dropped. One by one, the accusers walked away (John 8:9).

Jesus did not excuse the woman's sin, but He refused to condemn her publicly. "Then neither do I condemn you," Jesus declared. "Go now and leave your life of sin" (John 8:11). Mercy led the way, followed by a call to transformation. In that moment, Jesus showed that judgment rooted in pride has no place in the Kingdom of God.

The Plank and the Speck

This was not the only time Jesus spoke about judgment. Later, He addressed it directly, knowing how easily the human heart drifts toward comparison and condemnation.

"Do not judge, or you too will be judged" (Matthew 7:1).

Jesus knew how quickly people form opinions based on appearances. How easily we judge others by how they look, where they live, what they own, or where they come from. But judgment is the opposite of loving our neighbor, and it slowly hardens the heart.

To make His point unmistakable, Jesus asked, "Why do you look at the speck of sawdust in your brother's eye and pay no attention to the plank in your own eye?" (Matthew 7:3).

The image is intentionally exaggerated. No one can see clearly enough to help another while ignoring their own brokenness. The issue is not discernment, but hypocrisy. Jesus teaches that correction, when it is needed, must come from humility and grace, never from a place of superiority (Matthew 7:5).

The Parable of the Pharisee and the Tax Collector

Jesus continued this teaching through a parable. He told of two men who went up to the temple to pray, one a Pharisee and the other a tax collector (Luke 18:10).

Many in Israel measured their worth by status, influence, and outward obedience. From the outside, their lives appeared complete. Yet Jesus knew that outward appearance did not always reflect the condition of the heart.

The Pharisee stood by himself and prayed, thanking God he was not like other people, robbers, evildoers, adulterers, or even like the tax collector standing nearby (Luke 18:11). The tax collector, however, stood at a distance. He would not even look up to heaven, but beat his chest and said, "God, have mercy on me, a sinner" (Luke 18:13).

Jesus concluded by saying that it was this man, the humble one, who went home justified before God, not the religious leader. "For all those who exalt themselves will be humbled, and those who humble themselves will be exalted" (Luke 18:14). Once again, Jesus revealed that God is far more concerned with the posture of the heart than the appearance of righteousness.

Why This Story Matters

Throughout His ministry, Jesus consistently spoke to the condition of the heart. He taught us to love our neighbors as ourselves. Yet the world around us often teaches something very different.

We are constantly shown who is celebrated and who is overlooked, what is considered impressive and what is not. Over time, these messages can quietly influence how we see others and even how we see ourselves. Without realizing it, our hearts can begin to drift away from compassion.

When we start measuring people by outward appearances or comparing ourselves to others, we may slowly close ourselves off to the grace God wants to pour into our lives. But Jesus never speaks these truths to shame us. He speaks them to invite us back into a life where we are no longer weighed down by guilt or comparison.

Jesus invites us to lay our stones down, to let go of our urge to judge or condemn others, and to allow God to reshape how we see, speak, and love.

A Prayer to End

Dear Jesus, thank You for showing us through Your life how we are meant to live — lives filled with love, mercy, and grace. Help us resist the urge to judge others, regardless of who they are, where they come from, or what they look like. Shape our hearts to see beyond what this world says is important, so we may build relationships rooted in Your truth, not our own understanding. As we grow in our faith, reveal our shortcomings and give us the strength to overcome them, so we may be used as an instrument in Your plan to bring others into Your Kingdom. Amen.

Bible References

John 8 — Mercy over condemnation
Matthew 7 — Examine yourself first
Luke 18 — God looks at the heart

READING 24

In the Year of Our Lord, ~AD 32

The Prodigal Son

A Gathering Crowd of Faithful Listeners

One day, Jesus taught a group of people with very different backgrounds and motives. Some were tax collectors, and others were known sinners whom people in the community often looked down on. Others were religious leaders, Pharisees, and teachers of the law, men who prided themselves on following and enforcing every religious rule.

The Pharisees' bitterness toward Jesus steadily grew, and now they had a reason to grumble again, this time about the type of people Jesus welcomed. "This man welcomes sinners," they said, "and eats with them" (Luke 15:1–2). Jesus knew exactly what they were thinking. So, to better help the people in attendance understand what God's heart is really like, He shared a story. It's one of His most famous parables, and it still speaks deeply to those who hear it today.

The Prodigal — A Son Who Walked Away

There once was a man who was blessed to have two sons. The younger son came to his father and demanded, "Father, give me my share of the estate." This was a shocking and selfish request. The son was basically telling his father, "I don't want to wait until you die, I want your money now" (Luke 15:11–12).

Even though it must have hurt and disappointed the father to hear his son talk this way to him, the father agreed and gave the younger son his inheritance.

Soon after, the younger son packed up all he owned, left his father's home, and moved to a faraway country. He wanted to live his life his own way. No more rules or responsibilities now that he was out of his father's home. At first, everything was new, fun, and exciting. He spent his money irresponsibly on wine, food, and whatever else his heart desired. But then the money was gone — all of it.

A short time later, a famine devastated the land, and suddenly, the son was alone, hungry, and poor. He had absolutely nothing left but the clothes on his back. Eventually, he landed a job feeding pigs, but his situation was still bad. One day while working, he was so hungry, he even fantasized about eating the pigs' food (Luke 15:13–16).

Desperate, he thought, "How many of my father's hired servants have food to spare, and here I am starving to death! I will set out and go back to my father and say to him: 'Father, I have sinned against heaven and against you. I am no longer worthy to be called your son.'" So, he left his job and started the long walk back home (Luke 15:17–19).

A Father Who Quickly Forgave

While the son was still off in the distance, his father saw him. He had been watching, hoping, praying that one day, maybe his son would return. His heart was full of love and compassion, and he ran out to greet his son.

He threw his arms around him and kissed him. The son, caught off guard by his father's affection, began his speech: "Father, I have sinned against heaven and against you. I am no longer worthy to be called your son."

But the father interrupted him and told his servants, "Quick! Bring the best robe and put it on him. Put a ring on his finger and sandals on his feet. Bring the fattened calf and kill it. Let's have a feast and celebrate. For this son of mine was dead and is alive again; he was lost and is found." They all rejoiced and celebrated his return (Luke 15:20–24).

A Brother's Heart Revealed

But not everyone in the house was happy. The older brother, who had stayed and worked hard on the farm, was surprised to hear the celebration. He was angry when he learned what was happening; he refused to go inside to greet his brother.

His father came outside to speak to him and pleaded with his older son to join the celebration. But he refused and said, "Look! All these years I've been slaving for you and never disobeyed your orders. Yet you never gave me even a young goat so I could celebrate with my friends. But when this son of yours who has squandered your property with prostitutes comes home, you kill the fattened calf for him!"

The father replied softly, "My son, you are always with me, and everything I have is yours. But we had to celebrate and be glad, because this brother of yours was dead and is alive again; he was lost and is found" (Luke 15:25–32).

Why This Story Matters

In today's world, it is easy to compare our lives to others. The number of likes or followers, paired with carefully curated images online, can distort our view of life and leave us feeling as though we are missing something. When we constantly see what others appear to have, it can stir up impatience and convince us that happiness is found somewhere else and that we should have it now.

That same longing is reflected in the younger son's story. He is not content with the life he has been given. He does not want to wait. He demands his inheritance immediately, believing it will lead to a better, fuller life. Whether he realizes it or not, his choice represents a life turned away from God, driven by personal desire and temporary satisfaction. And as the story shows, when we chase life on our own terms and leave God out of our decisions, we often end up broken, lost, and far from home.

The father represents God, who never stops watching and waiting. The moment the son turns back, the father runs to him with open arms. There are no conditions, no lectures, and no demands to earn his way back, only grace, restoration, and love.

The older brother represents another danger we all face. He followed the rules, but his heart never embraced mercy. He measured love by fairness instead of grace. Yet the story does not end with rejection. Like the father in the parable, God meets us with compassion when we return to Him. He does not shame us or keep a record of our failures. He simply welcomes us home, reminding us that His love is a gift freely given and has been waiting for us all along.

A Prayer to End

Dear God, thank You for loving us like the prodigal father, waiting for us patiently, giving us space and time to figure things out, and running toward us with joy when we do. Help us remember that Your grace and love are for everyone, not just those who appear to "have it all figured out." Give us hearts that support, forgive, welcome, and celebrate those all over the world who return home to You. Amen.

Bible References

Luke 15 — Jesus welcomes sinners; the prodigal son leaves and returns home; the older brother's response and the father's mercy

In the Year of Our Lord, ~AD 32

Mary Anoints Jesus' Feet with Perfume

A Family Touched by Resurrection

Jesus traveled to Bethany to visit dear friends who lived there. Among them was Lazarus, a man Jesus deeply loved, along with his two sisters, Mary and Martha. Their home was often a place of welcome and rest during Jesus' ministry.

Before this visit, Jesus had visited Lazarus another time, but under much different circumstances. Lazarus was severely ill, so his sisters sent a message to Jesus to notify Him of their brother's condition. They believed He could help. Even though Jesus loved Lazarus, He delayed His visit, knowing a greater display of God's glory was yet to unfold. By the time He arrived in Bethany, Lazarus had died and been in a tomb for four days.

Both Mary and Martha were heartbroken. Moved by their sorrow, Jesus wept also. Then, as He stood before the tomb, He called Lazarus out, and Lazarus came back to life (John 11:43–44).

This miracle stunned everyone. Lazarus became a living sign of the power Jesus possessed. So, when Jesus returned to Bethany just six days before Passover, the townspeople welcomed Him with open arms, and His friends prepared a special dinner in His honor.

But not everyone was happy about His growing popularity. Some told the religious leaders about Jesus raising Lazarus from the dead, and the news angered them. They began to plot against Jesus, determined to bring Him down.

A Fragrant Gift of Worship

Meanwhile, Martha, always the homemaker, prepared the food for the feast they had arranged to honor Jesus. Lazarus, once dead, now relaxed at the table and sat beside Him. And Mary, the quiet sister with a heart full of gratitude, carried a small jar of expensive perfume into the room.

Without saying a word, Mary knelt beside Jesus, weeping, her tears wetting His feet; she wiped them with her hair and poured perfume on them (Luke 7:38). The aroma filled the entire house.

Mary's gesture was one of deep love and humble worship. Jesus brought her brother back to life, and Mary wasn't waiting another second for the opportunity to thank Him. She simply gave Him the best she had while she had the chance.

Judas' Voice of Disapproval

But not everyone at the table appreciated Mary's act of love. Judas Iscariot, one of Jesus' twelve disciples, spoke with sharp criticism. "Why this waste of perfume? It could have been sold for more than a year's wages and the money given to the poor" (Mark 14:4–5).

On the surface, his question seemed considerate, thoughtful even. But Judas didn't care about the plight of the poor. His words covered up the real issue at hand: his greedy heart. Judas was responsible for carrying the disciples' moneybag, but his love of money began to corrupt his heart (John 12:6). He resented Mary's actions because he knew her expensive gift could have been used to help himself.

Jesus Defends What Others Miss

Jesus, who saw through every layer of Judas' deceptive heart, stood up for Mary. "Leave her alone," He said. "Why are you bothering her? She has done a beautiful thing to me" (Mark 14:6). Jesus didn't just defend her, He honored her. He saw her beautiful heart, her humility, and her courage.

While others whispered and judged, Jesus received her offering with tenderness and gratitude.

Why This Story Matters

This story challenges us to pause and reflect. Are we offering Jesus our minds and our hearts, or just our outward appearances? Do we worship with open faith like Mary, or do we calculate each step like Judas?

Mary's act was humble and deeply personal, yet risky. She gave generously out of love because she knew who Jesus was and what He had done for her family. She knew some at the table might be upset with her gesture, but she didn't care. Her worship wasn't planned; it was spontaneous and from the heart. And Jesus cherished her for it.

Judas, however, outwardly chose to follow Jesus, but his heart had grown distant and dark. He covered his greed with nice-sounding words, but his motives were selfish and hollow.

Jesus doesn't care about outward appearances. His focus is the true condition of our hearts. Like Mary, when our actions, motives, and prayers show a genuine love for Jesus, He receives them with pride and joy.

A Prayer to End

Dear God, thank You for reminding us that our hearts are what is most important to You. Help us love You like Mary did, freely, humbly, and regardless of what others think. Protect us from the slow drift into selfishness and the importance we place on outward appearances. Let our worship be from the heart — real and never routine. Teach us to give You our best and not our leftovers. You are worthy of it all. Amen.

Bible References

John 11 — Jesus raises Lazarus from the dead
Luke 7 — Mary anoints Jesus with perfume in Bethany
Matthew 26 — Judas questions Mary's gift
Mark 14 — Jesus defends Mary's act of worship
John 12 — Judas' motive exposed

In the Year of Our Lord, ~AD 32

Judas Plots to Betray Jesus

A Crowded City and a Brewing Storm

It was the week of Passover, and Jerusalem was filled with people from all over Israel and Judah. Pilgrims, faithful Jews who traveled from areas such as Syria, Asia Minor, Greece, and Egypt, arrived to remember how God once rescued His people from slavery in Egypt. The streets were busy, the Temple was full, and each day Jesus taught the people, sharing stories and speaking openly about the Kingdom of God.

But underneath it all, a quiet storm was brewing.

The religious leaders had been watching Jesus closely for a while now. His words stirred the people's hearts and minds, but at the same time disturbed the balance of power. Day after day, Jesus revealed hearts, exposed hypocrisy, and reminded the people that God desired mercy, not just tradition. Eventually, the religious leaders had heard enough. They were no longer just irritated but were determined to get rid of Him. They just needed to find the right opportunity. And they did. Judas Iscariot, one of Jesus' very own, was secretly starting to question everything.

A Disciple's Dangerous Plan

Judas had walked closely with Jesus and the other disciples for three years. He witnessed many miracles, heard the parables, and cared for people all over the region. Judas also handled the money used to support their mission.

At first glance, managing the finances seemed like an honor to Judas. But over time, greed began to take its toll on him. He carried the disciples' moneybag and often helped himself to what was inside (John 12:6). What started off as small acts of dishonesty grew into deeper corruption.

Judas also paid close attention to Jesus; he could tell things were changing. Jesus spoke more and more about His upcoming death. He warned His disciples that suffering was coming their way. Jesus also said He would be handed over to His enemies.

Judas may have started to wonder: "Maybe Jesus isn't the Messiah after all. Maybe He's just an ordinary man. What will happen to me when all of this falls apart?" Instead of having faith and surrendering to the truth, Judas started looking out for his own interests and making selfish decisions. He chose personal gain over loyalty to Jesus.

He approached the chief priests and asked a chilling question, "What are you willing to give me if I deliver him over to you?" They offered him a bounty of thirty silver coins, the same price paid for a slave. Judas accepted it. And from that moment on, he watched for the right opportunity to betray Jesus (Matthew 26:14–16).

Knowing His Betrayer

Judas didn't walk away from his role as a disciple. He stayed with the group and continued traveling and eating beside them, all while carrying this terrible secret. He followed Jesus publicly, but his plot to betray Him darkened his heart.

Even before Judas made his deal with the chief priests, Jesus already knew his wicked plans. These events were mentioned in the Scriptures and outlined the coming betrayal. The psalmist wrote: "Even my close friend, someone I trusted, one who shared my bread, has turned against me" (Psalm 41:9).

Although He knew his plot, Jesus didn't push Judas away. He didn't want to shame him in front of the others, so He walked with him until the very end. He even allowed Judas to sit at His side for the Last Supper.

Jesus loved Judas, even when betrayal was already put into motion.

Why This Story Matters

Judas' story is sad but also serves as a warning. He was chosen and walked beside Jesus, the living God. He witnessed Jesus' miracles, healing, and teaching firsthand. He heard truth from the actual source of truth, and still, he stumbled.

"Why?" you might ask. Because deep down, Judas still lived life with an earthly mindset. He still prioritized money, status, and security. And when it appeared Jesus' ministry would end in death instead of triumph, Judas tried to seize control. Rather than trusting God's plan, he made his own plan and cut a deal with those who hated Jesus. Judas didn't believe he was with the King, but with a man whose time was running out.

This story reminds us of the danger of appearing close to Jesus on the outside while remaining far from Him in our hearts. It's possible to hear the truth and still choose our own way. When left unchecked, our small compromises can grow into major betrayals.

A Prayer to End

Dear God, thank You for showing us the complete truth of this story, not just the betrayal for coins, but the sorrow behind it. Guard our hearts, Lord, from selfishness, greed, and doubt that pull our focus away from You. Keep us from going through the motions on the outside while we are drifting further from You on the inside. Teach us to seek You honestly, each day, to grow in a faith that is genuine and real, and not for show. Amen.

Bible References

John 12 — Judas' greed revealed as he steals from the money bag
Matthew 26 — Judas agrees to betray Jesus for thirty silver coins
Psalm 41 — Prophecy of betrayal by a close friend

In the Year of Our Lord, ~AD 33

Jesus' Joyful Return to Jerusalem

The Road to Jerusalem

The long journey was almost over. Jesus and His disciples made their way toward Jerusalem, the great city where Jews from all over the land were gathering to celebrate the Passover. This festival was a celebration to remind those in attendance of how God delivered His people from slavery in Egypt long ago. Each year, the city was filled with excitement, but this year felt different. News spread everywhere about Jesus' works, His miracles, His teachings, and the way He had brought a man, Lazarus, back from the dead (John 11:43–44).

As they approached the Mount of Olives, Jesus paused and gave two of His disciples instructions: "Go to the village ahead of you, and at once you will find a donkey tied there, with her colt by her. Untie them and bring them to me. If anyone says anything to you, say that the Lord needs them and he will send them right away" (Matthew 21:2–3).

The disciples did exactly as they were told. When they came into the village, they saw the animals tied to a tree just as Jesus had described. As they began to untie them, the owner called out, "Why are you untying the colt?" (Luke 19:33). The disciples responded just as Jesus had told them to: "The Lord needs it" (Luke 19:34). The owner allowed them to go on their way, and they returned with the donkey and its colt.

They put their cloaks across the donkey's back, and Jesus sat on it. This act fulfilled an old prophecy that was written five hundred years earlier by the prophet Zechariah: "See, your king comes to you … lowly and riding on a donkey" (Zechariah 9:9). As they saw Jesus riding into town, they shouted and screamed with joy. The crowds that arrived early began to lay their coats and palm branches over the road. It was like a parade for a king (Matthew 21:7–8).

The palm branches were more than decoration; they were a national symbol of victory and hope. In the past, after a great military win, people welcomed the Jewish commanders home by waving palm branches in the air. So, the palm branches spread on the ground to welcome Jesus meant the people believed He would conquer their enemies. Today, palm branches are burned and the ashes used to mark the sign of the cross on a Catholic believer's forehead, carrying a simple but deep message: "For dust you are, and to dust you will return" (Genesis 3:19).

The Crowd Celebrates a King

All the people shouted, "Hosanna to the Son of David! Blessed is he who comes in the name of the Lord!" (Matthew 21:9). Hosanna was a term used as a cry for salvation. Many believed Jesus was the Savior they had been promised, the Messiah who would free Israel once and for all from tyranny. But they were thinking about freedom from Rome, not freedom from sin and wickedness.

For years, the Jewish people had lived under Roman authority. Before that, they were ruled by the Greeks, before that the Syrians, and so on. They were tired of being ruled by foreign nations. So, when they saw Jesus ride into Jerusalem, they hoped He was the kind of Savior who would destroy all of their enemies and take back their lands.

But that's not why He came.

The Pharisees didn't like hearing those in the crowd shout for Jesus. "Teacher," they said, "rebuke your disciples!" But Jesus replied, "I tell you, if they keep quiet, the stones will cry out" (Luke 19:39–40). It seemed like the whole world had been waiting for Jesus' arrival, and nothing could stop him.

Tears Shed for Jerusalem

As the road twisted and the city finally came into view, Jesus did something very unexpected. He wept (Luke 19:41). The crowd cheered, but His soul ached. "If you, even you, had only known on this day what would bring you peace," He whispered, "but now it is hidden from your eyes" (Luke 19:42).

Jesus knew many in the crowd didn't understand the purpose of His mission. They hoped for a king to change their daily circumstances, but He came to change their hearts. Also, He knew those cheering for Him today would be the same ones who would soon turn away. Still, He kept going because He loved them.

Why This Story Matters

As Jesus entered Jerusalem riding on a donkey, the crowd shouted with excitement. The people had long prayed for God to send a Messiah who would defeat Israel's enemies and make right the wrongs their families had endured for generations. They imagined a warrior king arriving with armor and a sword, ready to overthrow Rome, punish their oppressors, and restore Israel's power and glory.

They wanted a strong conqueror, not a humble servant. But Jesus did not come to overthrow earthly kingdoms. He came to defeat sin.

This story reminds us that God's plans are often very different from our expectations. The people were looking for immediate rescue from their circumstances, while God was carrying out a far greater plan, one that would bring eternal redemption. Jesus came not only to save people from enemies on the outside, but from the brokenness that lives within the human heart.

This moment invites us to pause and reflect on how we pray. Like the crowd, our prayers often focus on relief from our immediate troubles, worries, and hardships. And God welcomes those prayers. But this story invites us to pray with greater humility, trusting that we do not see the full picture. As we seek God's help in our trials, we can also ask for wisdom, patience, and clarity to understand how our circumstances might be used for good and for the growth of His kingdom.

May our prayers grow beyond what we want fixed right now and instead reflect a desire to be part of God's greater story, trusting that His plans are always bigger, wiser, and more loving than our own.

A Prayer to End

Dear Jesus, thank You for being exactly the King we needed. When we look for quick fixes or easy answers, remind us that You came to bring lasting peace. Open our eyes to see You clearly, and show us how to follow You, not with our own plans in mind, but with faith in Yours. May we live our lives by praising You with our actions, and not just our words. Amen.

Bible References

John 11 — Jesus raises Lazarus from the dead
Matthew 21 — Jesus rides into Jerusalem on a donkey
Luke 19 — Jesus enters Jerusalem and weeps over the city
Zechariah 9 — Prophecy of the King coming on a donkey
Genesis 3 — From dust we came, to dust we will return

Pause & Reflect — Transformation

Hearts Transformed

It is easy to become focused on things that bring us happiness, recognition, or approval from others. We can begin to measure our worth by what we own, how we appear, or how many people admire us. But Jesus' teachings invite us into a different way of living, one that transforms us from the inside out rather than focusing on outward appearance.

Transformation requires consistency. When we live one way in front of certain people and another way when no one is watching, it reveals areas where our faith is still maturing. Jesus calls us to live with integrity, allowing our faith to shape who we are in every setting, not just the ones that are most visible.

As we begin to change the way we speak, listen, and love others, our hearts are transformed. We grow more aware of God's will and purpose for our lives. And when our lives reflect that change, others begin to notice. They may ask questions about our faith, not because of what we say, but because of how we live, whether at work, in the classroom, or on the sports field.

Memory Verse

"Love the Lord your God with all your heart and with all your soul and with all your mind. Love your neighbor as yourself." — Matthew 22:37–39

Questions to Consider

Do the things we acquire or the gifts we receive ever cause us to measure our worth by comparison to others?

In what areas of our lives do we sense the Lord is working to transform our hearts?

A Prayer to End

Dear Jesus, thank You for sharing Your story with us so we can understand what it means to have transformed hearts. As our hearts are changed, help us better hear the purpose God has for our lives. Guide us as we reflect on the things we may be holding on to that keep us from becoming the people You are calling us to be. Give us the strength and courage to overcome our weaknesses and to live with faith and integrity. Amen.

In the Year of Our Lord, ~AD 33

The Tenants; The Seven Woes

A Confrontation in the Temple

Jesus entered the Temple and, for the second time, found tradesmen conducting business. Upon seeing this, He again flipped the tables of the merchants, driving out the money changers who continued to cheat the people and turn a place of prayer and worship into a place of profit (Matthew 21:12–13).

It was Jesus' final week in Jerusalem. The Temple was crowded, filled with pilgrims from all over the region who had come to celebrate the Passover festival. Most of the people gathered to worship, but something else stirred in the hearts of the religious leaders that day — anger, pride, and a growing hatred of Jesus because He continued to challenge their authority.

Jesus came to the Temple to teach those who sought truth and were willing to learn from Him. Meanwhile, the Pharisees, Sadducees, and teachers of the law hoped to trap Him with questions and discredit Him in front of the crowd. But Jesus did not waver. He spoke calmly to everyone present in the Temple that day, sharing stories and warnings that could not be ignored (Matthew 21:23-27).

The Parable of the Tenants

Jesus shared a parable with those around Him, one that pierced their pride and revealed the truth of their hearts.

"There was a landowner who planted a vineyard. He put a wall around it, dug a winepress in it and built a watchtower. Then he rented the vineyard to some farmers and moved to another place. When the harvest time approached, he sent his servants to the tenants to collect the fruit … [but] they beat one, killed another, and stoned a third.

"Then he sent other servants to them, more than the first time, and the tenants treated them the same way. Last of all, he sent his son to them. 'They will respect my son.' But when the tenants saw the son, they said to each other, 'This is the heir. Come, let's kill him and take his inheritance.' So, they took him and threw him out of the vineyard and killed him" (Matthew 21:33–39).

Jesus then asked the crowd, "Therefore, when the owner of the vineyard comes, what will he do to those tenants?" The people replied, "He will bring those wretches to a wretched end, and he will rent the vineyard to other tenants, who will give him his share of the crop at harvest time." Jesus looked at them and said, "The stone the builders rejected has become the cornerstone … Therefore, I tell you that the kingdom of God will be taken away from you and given to a people who will produce its fruit" (Matthew 21:40–43).

The religious leaders stared angrily at Jesus. They knew He was talking about them. They were the tenants who had rejected the prophets sent by God and would soon reject and crucify His Son. But they were afraid to arrest Jesus because of the size of the crowd that followed Him.

The Seven Woes

Later that same day, Jesus spoke directly to the Pharisees and other teachers of the law, giving them seven powerful warnings known as the seven woes. They were harsh, honest, and full of sadness. Jesus was angry that these religious leaders led people away from God. He said:

"Woe to you" for making it harder for people to find God, not easier.

"Woe to you" for caring more about gaining followers rather than leading them to truth.

"Woe to you" for manipulating truth to benefit you.

"Woe to you" for focusing on rules but ignoring justice, mercy, and faithfulness.

"Woe to you" for looking clean on the outside but ignoring greed and selfishness on the inside.

"Woe to you" for looking faithful but having hearts that are corrupt.

"Woe to you" for honoring God's messengers of the past but rejecting God's message in the present (Matthew 23:13–37).

Jesus did not say these words to shame them but to save them, before the opportunity to be part of God's Kingdom passed them by.

Why This Story Matters

In the parable of the tenants, Jesus confronts a dangerous belief held by the religious leaders: that heritage and tradition guaranteed their spot in God's Kingdom. They believed the

Kingdom belonged to them simply because of who they were and where they came from. But Jesus showed they trusted their position more than they trusted God.

When Jesus declared the Kingdom of God would be taken away and given to a people who would produce fruit, He was not speaking of one nation replacing another. He was revealing that God's Kingdom belongs to those who trust Him, obey Him, and live out a genuine faith. The issue was not identity; it was the heart. The tenants did not lose the vineyard because they were weak; they lost it because they rejected the owner and killed the son.

This moment marked a turning point. God's plan to restore people back to Himself, first entrusted to Israel, would now be opened fully to all who believe, Jews and Gentiles (non-Jews) alike. The true people of God would no longer be defined by ancestry or religious authority, but by repentance, belief in Jesus, and lives that reflect His truth.

The seven woes that followed served as a warning. Knowledge of Scripture without humility leads to blindness. Religious activity without obedience leads to emptiness. And authority without love leads to judgment. Jesus did not condemn faithfulness; He condemned fruitlessness.

This story challenges us to look honestly at our faith. The Kingdom of God is not something we inherit or claim by title, but something we receive and live out through obedience and trust in Jesus.

A Prayer to End

Dear God, thank You for sending messengers to guide us, especially Your Son. We are sorry for the times we have ignored Your voice or closed our hearts to Your greater purpose. Help us come to You each day, trusting in Your strength rather than our own understanding. Teach us to live in a way that reflects Your love, so others may see You in how we care, how we serve, and how we treat every person around us, no matter who they are. Amen.

Bible References

Matthew 21 — Parable of the tenants
Matthew 23 — The seven woes

In the Year of Our Lord, ~AD 33

The Widow's Offering; The Humble Guest

Tension Swelling in the City

The city of Jerusalem was alive with activity, and the tension between Jesus and the religious leaders increased every day. Just days earlier, Jesus arrived in Jerusalem riding a donkey, fulfilling prophecy as the crowds cried out, "Hosanna! Blessed is He who comes in the name of the Lord!" (Mark 11:9). That joy and hope bumped up against the chief priests' suspicion and unrest. Jesus questioned their authority and teachings and told parables that pointed directly to the corruption of their hearts.

Now, once again, Jesus preached inside the Temple courts and spoke to those in the crowd about the religious leaders' shortcomings: "Watch out for the teachers of the law. They like to walk around in flowing robes and be greeted with respect … They devour widows' houses and for a show make lengthy prayers. These men will be punished most severely" (Mark 12:38–40).

Jesus wasn't afraid to expose the truth. He held the religious leaders, with their outward holiness, accountable for their selfishness and poor treatment of others. They loved having the best seats and being seen and greeted with respect. But their hearts had drifted far from God and the people they claimed to serve.

The Woman Who Gave Out of Her Poverty

Then, Jesus and His disciples made their way to an area near the Temple treasury. This area, called the Court of Women, had thirteen trumpet-shaped bowls used to collect offerings. Wealthy worshipers made their way to these containers and dropped in large sums of money (Mark 12:41). The sound of coins echoed throughout the Temple courts, and with each weighty donation, onlookers nodded in approval. Everyone in town knew who the wealthy were, and the wealthy enjoyed the attention they received when they gave.

But Jesus was captivated by something completely different.

He saw a poor widow come forward to give. She didn't wear expensive clothing or come from wealth. Her steps were slow and quiet, and hardly anyone there noticed her. Out of her coin purse, she withdrew two small copper coins, known as lepta, the smallest coins in circulation (Mark 12:42). When she dropped them into the bowl, they barely made a sound. No one turned their heads. No one paid any attention to her at all. She came and left unseen.

Unseen by everyone except for Jesus.

He quickly called His disciples over and said, "Truly I tell you, this poor widow has put more into the treasury than all the others. They all gave out of their wealth; but she, out of her poverty, put in everything, all she had to live on" (Mark 12:43–44).

It wasn't the amount of her giving that amazed Jesus; it was the depth of her faith. The others donated money based on what they could spare. She gave money she could not afford to give, but she gave it joyfully anyway.

The Wedding Table and the Humble Guest

One day, Jesus was invited to dine at the home of a prominent Pharisee. As the guests arrived, He noticed how they hurried to claim the seats closest to the head table, the places of highest honor that showed off a person's importance. Seeing this, Jesus shared a parable to teach them about true humility (Luke 14:7).

"When someone invites you to a wedding feast, do not take the place of honor, for a person more distinguished than you may have been invited. If so, the host who invited both of you will come and say to you, 'Give this person your seat' … [so instead one should] take the lowest place, so that when your host comes, he will say to you, 'Friend, move up to a better place'" (Luke 14:8–10).

Jesus wasn't giving social advice about how a person should choose their seat. He was sharing how the Kingdom of God works. In a world that celebrates pride, status, and visibility, Jesus honored those who lived with humility, those who did the right things for the right reasons. That is what truly honors God.

Why This Story Matters

The widow who gave her last two coins and the guest who took the low seat have something beautiful in common. Both lived with humble, faithful hearts. They weren't trying to be noticed or impress anyone. They simply did what was good and just in the eyes of the Lord, regardless of whether anyone else saw it.

That should be a lesson for us all.

God doesn't measure our faith by how openly we serve, how much we give, or how good we look. We can't earn our way into heaven, or into God's good graces, by simply checking religious boxes. His focus is on the condition of our hearts. He sees the person who chooses humility when arrogance would be easier. He sees the one who gives quietly when admiration would feel better. Jesus promises that those who lower themselves and stay humble — giving God the glory and living faithful lives — will one day be honored by God himself.

In a world filled with status and applause, it's easy to think our value comes from what others think. But Jesus shares something far more powerful. God sees what everyone else misses: quiet acts of faith, humble sacrifices, and small, costly offerings made with love.

A Prayer to End

Dear God, thank You for seeing the small things the world overlooks and discounts. Thank You for sharing with us that it's not the size of our gift but the heart behind it You care about most. Help us give generously, faithfully, and humbly, just as the widow did. Help us be okay with taking the lowest seat, serving without applause, and giving You all the glory when we are recognized. Amen.

Bible References

Mark 11 — Jesus enters Jerusalem
Mark 12 — The widow's offering
Luke 14 — Parable on humility

In the Year of Our Lord, ~AD 33

Jesus Predicts the Temple's Destruction

A Sobering Prophecy

Jesus spent most of His week teaching in Jerusalem, often inside the Temple courts. The Temple was the pride of the entire Jewish people, impressive, beautiful, and sacred. It stood on top of Mount Zion. Its limestone and gold-covered walls glimmered in the sun, a true wonder of the ancient world, and pilgrims came from near and far to see it.

But not all of those who admired the Temple truly honored God. Many of the religious leaders cared more about their status within the Temple than justice, mercy, or truth. Many people in the community placed their faith in the building itself rather than in the God who once filled it with His presence and glory.

After Jesus and His disciples left the Temple for the day, one of them paused, wide-eyed with admiration. "Look, Teacher! What massive stones! What magnificent buildings!" (Mark 13:1). Jesus turned around and replied with stinging words: "Do you see all these great buildings? Not one stone here will be left on another; every one will be thrown down" (Mark 13:2).

These words were shocking to hear, but the prophets from long ago had warned that if the hearts of the people didn't turn back to God, even the most sacred places would be destroyed. For example, the prophet Micah declared:

"Zion will be plowed like a field, Jerusalem will become a heap of rubble, the Temple hill a mound overgrown with thickets" (Micah 3:12).

Jesus echoed the truths shared by the prophets thousands of years earlier. He saw the Temple was turned into a place of national pride and rituals, not one of worship and repentance.

A Quiet Warning on the Mount of Olives

After Jesus and His disciples left the city, they crossed into the Kidron Valley and rested on the Mount of Olives, gazing back in the distance at the Temple. The view was amazing, but the moment was heavy.

Peter, James, John, and Andrew approached Jesus in private and asked Him about His earlier prediction, "Tell us, when will these things happen? And what will be the sign that they are about to be fulfilled?" (Mark 13:4). Jesus' answer was long but full of meaning. Not only did He talk about the coming destruction of the Temple and the city of Zion, but He spoke of the days to come, including the challenges all believers would face in the future. "Watch out that no one deceives you," He said. "Many will come in my name, claiming, 'I am he,' and will deceive many" (Mark 13:5–6).

He warned of false messiahs and spoke of brutal wars, natural disasters, and religious persecution the disciples would face after He was gone. He said society would hate them and other believers because of His name. Even their own families would betray them. Still, Jesus urged them to stand firm in their faith.

"Everyone will hate you because of me, but the one who stands firm to the end will be saved" (Mark 13:13).

Jesus did not share these warnings to frighten His disciples but to prepare them for the distractions and deceptions meant to lead them away from the truth. That's why He told them again and again to "Be on guard! Be alert!" (Mark 13:33).

Even today, we face many of the same distractions. Fame, fear, comfort, pride, laziness, complacency, and empty religion all try to pull our attention away from Jesus.

Why This Story Matters

Jesus' prediction about the future destruction of the Temple was not just about history or architecture; it was about where people placed their faith. Many trusted stone walls and sacred buildings more than the living God. But Jesus offered them something far greater, a Kingdom that would never fall.

Every word Jesus spoke came true when the Romans destroyed the Temple in Jerusalem in AD 70. Not one stone was left standing. The Temple was gone, but Jesus' new church was just beginning to grow. What appeared to be the end of everything familiar became the beginning of something eternal.

Just as the early believers faced opposition and persecution, followers of Christ today are tested by a world that often misunderstands, dismisses, or attempts to silence faith. We are made to feel as though belief should be kept private, our faith is outdated, or followers of Jesus are slowly fading away. But that is not the truth. God's Kingdom is alive and growing, and His people continue to stand firm, even when the world pushes back.

This story reminds us that our confidence does not come from what we see around us, but from what Jesus has already accomplished. The battle has been won. Christ has overcome the world. Our calling is not to retreat in fear, but to remain faithful, alert, and prayerful, keeping our eyes fixed on Him and trusting His Kingdom will endure forever.

A Prayer to End

Dear God, thank You for Jesus, our true Cornerstone, the One we can confidently build our lives, hopes, and dreams upon. Teach us to hear Your words above the noise and distractions that try to pull us away from You. Like a light tower, help us stay alert, ready, and awake, ready to receive Your good and holy plans for our lives. Strengthen us to share our faith confidently so others may come to know who You are. Amen.

Bible References

Mark 13 — Jesus predicts the destruction of the Temple and warns His disciples
Micah 3 — Prophecy about Zion being destroyed because of corruption

In the Year of Our Lord, ~AD 33

The Last Supper

Prepping the Upper Room

Evening had come, and upstairs in a quiet room in Jerusalem, the disciples sat together with Jesus, reflecting on all they had seen and heard that day. Over the last couple of years, this small group of men and their Teacher had traveled many miles, faced crowds, storms, and challenges, and shared many meals together. They were no longer just students following a leader; they were a family, growing in faith and learning to trust God and one another. Jesus knew His time with the disciples was coming to an end, and He wanted this night together to be one they would never forget.

He turned to Peter and John and told them, "Go and make preparations for us to eat the Passover. As you enter the city, a man carrying a jar of water will meet you. Follow him to the house that he enters, and say to the owner of the house, 'The Teacher asks: Where is the guest room, where I may eat the Passover with my disciples?' He will show you a large room upstairs, all furnished. Make preparations there" (Luke 22: 8–12).

Everything was exactly as Jesus said. The two disciples found the man, followed him into the home, and prepared everything. Later that evening, as the sun began to set, Jesus and the rest of the disciples arrived and joined them in the upper room (Mark 14:16–17).

Washing the Disciples' Feet

Before sitting down for dinner, Jesus stood up. Without saying a word, He took off His outer robe, placed a towel around His waist, and poured water into a bowl. Then, He surprised the disciples by kneeling beside them and washing their feet, one by one (John 13:4–5).

They were completely stunned. It was a servant's job to wash the feet of attending guests, not a job for their Teacher and Lord. When Jesus approached Peter, Peter said, "Lord, are you going to wash my feet?" (John 13:6).

Jesus answered, "You do not realize now what I am doing, but later you will understand." Peter shook his head in disagreement. "No," he said, "you shall never wash my feet." Jesus looked at him and said softly, "Unless I wash you, you have no part with me." After hearing that, Peter's heart softened. "Then, Lord, not just my feet, but my hands and my head as well!" (John 13:7–9).

When Jesus was done, He put on His outer robe again and returned to His place at the table. He said, "Do you understand what I have done for you? You call me 'Teacher' and 'Lord,' and rightly so, for that is what I am. Now that I, your Lord and Teacher, have washed your feet, you also should wash one another's feet. I have set you an example" (John 13:12–15).

Breaking Bread and Wine with the Disciples

As they sat around the table, the mood changed, and Jesus became quiet. "Very truly I tell you, one of you is going to betray me," He said (John 13:21).

The disciples looked at each other in shock. "Surely you don't mean me, Lord?" they asked Jesus one after the other. Judas, who had already negotiated with the Jewish religious leaders to betray Jesus, also asked, "Surely you don't mean me, Rabbi?" Jesus answered him, "You have said so" (Matthew 26:22–25).

Jesus then picked up a loaf of bread. He gave thanks, prayed, broke it, and handed it to them. "This is my body given up for you; do this in remembrance of me" (Luke 22:19).

After they finished eating, He took a cup of wine and looked at them all and said, "This is my blood of the covenant, which is poured out for many for the forgiveness of sins" (Matthew 26:28). They didn't fully understand Him at the time, but His words stayed with them forever.

Peter's Denial and Jesus' Warning

As the night ended, Jesus spoke again. "This very night you will all fall away on account of me" (Matthew 26:31). Peter spoke up in disbelief. "Even if all fall away on account of you, I never will!" (Matthew 26:33).

Jesus looked at him kindly and said, "Before the rooster crows, you will disown me three times." Peter replied, full of emotion. "Even if I have to die with you, I will never disown you." And the others quickly agreed (Matthew 26:34–35).

But Jesus knew what was waiting for Him: betrayal, denial, fear, and the cross. Yet, He stayed and shared this sacred meal to show them His love would never fail.

Why This Story Matters

The Last Supper with the disciples was not just a meal; it was a turning point. Together in that quiet room, Jesus showed the kind of love that kneels low, serves willingly, and humbles itself. Jesus washed their dirty feet. He offered them bread and wine. Even more, He gave them something they didn't realize they needed: the memory of His sweet words and the promise of His beautiful sacrifice.

When Jesus spoke of the one who would betray Him, each disciple quickly replied, "Surely not I, Lord?" Their response revealed how much confidence they still had in themselves rather than in Him. Instead of defending their own strength, the better response would have been, "Lord, give me the strength to stand for You, even when I'm weak."

They all wanted to be courageous. They all wanted to stay strong and faithful. But Jesus knew each of their weaknesses, and He still invited them to the table.

Let this be a reminder to each of us not to become overly confident in ourselves. It is a dangerous and lonely place when we build our lives on our own truth, our own strength, and our own understanding, instead of trusting the One who created everything.

A Prayer to End

Dear Jesus, help us remember the power of that night in a quiet room with your disciples, how You humbled Yourself to serve others, even as You prepared to suffer. Let that kind of love shape the way we treat and speak to others. When we face moments of fear or doubt, as Peter did, remind us, even on the days we fall short, You love us anyway. Amen.

Bible References

Luke 22 — The upper room and Passover preparations
Mark 14 — Jesus' disciples prepare the Passover
John 13 — Jesus washes the disciples' feet and predicts betrayal
Matthew 26 — The Last Supper and Peter's denial

Jesus' New Commandment

A Plan Put Into Action

While still in the upper room, the smell of bread and wine lingered in the air. The room had grown quiet and still. The previous laughter and stories had faded, replaced with a strong sense that something important was about to happen. Jesus had just washed the disciples' feet and spoken of His betrayal. Peter asked Jesus who would betray Him, and He answered, "It is the one to whom I will give this piece of bread when I have dipped it in the dish." Then He handed the bread to Judas Iscariot, who gladly took it (John 13:2–5, 21–26).

Judas left suddenly after taking the bread from Jesus, stepping out into the busy streets of Jerusalem. The other disciples didn't realize or fully understand why he had left. Some assumed he had gone to buy more food or give money to the poor, since he kept the group's money bag. But Jesus knew exactly what his plans were. Judas had agreed to turn Jesus over to the religious leaders. Historians believe that after leaving Jesus, Judas may have gone straight to the priests to alert them where He and his disciples could be found later that evening. In those days, the religious leaders were afraid to arrest Jesus in public because they feared the people's reaction. Judas offered them a quiet solution (John 13:27–30; Matthew 26:14–16).

Now, with Judas gone, only eleven disciples remained. As they sat together, Jesus smiled and looked around at His closest friends. They had walked hundreds of miles together, slept many nights under the stars, witnessed and performed miracles together, and become family. Jesus taught them how to pray, how to forgive, and how to trust God with everything they had. Yet, they still didn't completely understand what was about to take place in the next twenty-four hours (Luke 22:28–30; Matthew 26:31–32).

Jesus knew He didn't have much time left to be with them, and there was one very important thing they needed to hear. Not another miracle or a parable to remember, but something spoken directly from Jesus' heart. Something they would remember for the rest of their lives; even when fear tried to pull them apart, they would remember (John 13:33).

A New Command for a New World

He leaned toward them and said, "A new command I give you: Love one another. As I have loved you, so you must love one another" (John 13:34).

It wasn't the first time they heard Jesus proclaim this type of message. Earlier, during the Sermon on the Mount, Jesus had said things that amazed everyone. "You have heard that it was said, 'Love your neighbor and hate your enemy.' But I tell you, love your enemies and pray for those who persecute you" (Matthew 5:43–44).

He also had told them, "If anyone slaps you on the right cheek, turn to them the other cheek also" (Matthew 5:39), and "If anyone forces you to go one mile, go with them two miles" (Matthew 5:41). These words were hard to swallow at first. But Jesus painted a picture of a real love that went far beyond boundaries. One that gave, forgave, and restored.

This night felt different, though. Jesus' words carried a new sense of urgency. This wasn't teaching for the people; it was a personal call for those who would carry His message forward. Time was short, and Jesus needed them to understand, really understand, the kind of love that would carry them forward after He was gone (John 13:35, 15:9–12).

This love wasn't just about being kind. It was deeper than being polite or friendly. Jesus spoke about a love that served others without expecting anything in return. A love that forgave over and over again. A love that gave up authority, comfort, and even one's own life, so others could know hope. He wasn't asking for them to love the way the world loved. He was asking them to love the world like He loved (Philippians 2:5–8; John 15:13).

Then He said something very special: "By this, everyone will know that you are my disciples, if you love one another" (John 13:35).

The disciples looked at each other, quiet and thoughtful. Was it possible for people to really see Jesus by the way they treated one another? Would love be the standard that was more important than title, tradition, or belief? Jesus wasn't simply giving them words to remember. He gave them a mission to live their lives by, especially when He was no longer with them (1 John 3:18–19).

Why This Story Matters

And Jesus gave them a new command: "Love one another. As I have loved you, so you must love one another" (John 13:34).

The eleven disciples reflected on this moment later in their ministry and realized Jesus spoke these words to those who were flawed, not to those who were perfect. He spoke these words to His friends, who would scatter in fear soon. He spoke these words to Peter, who would even deny knowing Jesus. Still, Jesus loved them all to the end. That's what made this commandment so very different. It was love rooted in grace.

Jesus never asked His disciples to be the best speakers or the most perfect people. He didn't say people would know they were His followers based on how much they knew. He said His followers would be known by how much they loved.

And not just love for their friends, but the kind of love He had taught from the very beginning — love for one's enemies, a love that forgives, a love that gives without expecting anything in return.

On the night He washed the feet of His friends, He reminded them, and us, that real love costs something. But it's the clearest way the world will see who Jesus really is.

A Prayer to End

Jesus, thank You for showing us what real love looks like. It is not always easy, especially when someone has hurt us or when we are asked to love and pray for our enemies. But You loved even when it was hard and forgave when it wasn't easy. Help us love others like You do. May the love we show our neighbors and the lives we live reflect who You are, lives full of grace, humility, and kindness. Amen.

Bible References

John 13–15 — Jesus washes the disciples' feet, Judas leaves the upper room, and Jesus gives a new command to love one another

Matthew 26 — Judas agrees to betray Jesus; Jesus warns the disciples they will fall away

Luke 22 — Jesus prepares His disciples; Peter denies knowing Him

Matthew 5 — Sermon on the Mount teaching on love and forgiveness

Philippians 2 — Christ demonstrates love through humility

1 John 3 — Love must be shown through actions and truth

In the Year of Our Lord, ~AD 33

Words Shared Before the Garden

The Promise of a Helper

Night settled over Jerusalem, and the air grew quiet and still. Jesus had just given the disciples His new commandment — to love one another. Their hearts were hopeful but concerned. Something about this time together felt like a goodbye. But before they headed out to the garden, Jesus wanted to share more with them. Not bread or wine, but words that would serve as a guide.

Jesus sensed their worry, so He spoke words to comfort them. He didn't promise them ease, but He did give them truth: "Do not let your hearts be troubled. You believe in God; believe also in me" (John 14:1). He knew they would soon feel lost and alone without Him, so He made them a promise. "And I will ask the Father, and He will give you another advocate to help you and be with you forever — the Spirit of truth" (John 14:16–17). The disciples didn't understand His words initially, but eventually understood them completely. The Holy Spirit became their Advocate, their guide, protector, and faithful voice of everything Jesus said.

Jesus encouraged them when He said, "I will not leave you as orphans; I will come to you" (John 14:18). His love for them would never end, and His presence would still be with them by His Spirit.

The Story of the Vine and the Branches

They continued walking through the dark, quiet streets of Jerusalem, then up to a hillside near the Temple. Along the Temple walls, vines crept across and in between the stone and mortar. Jesus stopped, gently reached for a vine, and said, "I am the true vine, and my Father is the gardener" (John 15:1). He explained to His disciples that they were the branches, whose purpose was to bear good fruit through Him. "Remain in me, as I also remain in you. No branch can bear fruit by itself" (John 15:4).

His words were simple, but life-changing. The disciples didn't have to go through life on their own. They didn't have to understand every mystery He shared. They only had to trust Him, and as they did, He would give them the strength they needed in every situation.

A Truthful Warning and Fatherly Comfort

As they walked under the moonlight, Jesus' tone shifted. "If the world hates you, keep in mind that it hated me first" (John 15:18). He wanted to prepare them. He shared that some would reject them, insult them, and even seek to hurt them. He warned that others would even try to stop them from spreading His message.

Then, He explained why He told them these things: "I have told you this, so that when [the] time comes you will remember that I warned you" (John 16:4). He did not say this to scare them but to let them know what they'd face after He was gone.

Sorrow Will Turn to Joy

Jesus spoke softly about His upcoming departure; they would grieve, but their sorrow would not last forever. "You will grieve, but your grief will turn to joy" (John 16:20). He added that just as a woman feels pain during childbirth but rejoices after the baby arrives, the disciples would find joy on the other side of suffering.

Jesus also shared one of His most precious promises: "In that day you will ask in my name … the Father himself loves you because you have loved me" (John 16:26–27). The disciples would no longer be far away from God. Because of Jesus, each of them would have a direct relationship with the Father.

A Victory Before the Battle

The night was ending, and Jesus knew His death was imminent. Still, before His crucifixion, He gave His disciples one last word of encouragement. "In this world you will have trouble. But take heart! I have overcome the world" (John 16:33).

Why This Story Matters

Before Jesus walked into the Garden of Gethsemane, He gave His disciples something far more lasting than a meal or money; He gave them His heart. In these last few hours with His eleven disciples beside Him, He spoke words of truth and hope, sharing teachings He knew they would remember, understand, and one day pass on to others.

Jesus knew they were scared and their faith would be tested soon. Until now, Jesus had stood between His disciples and the religious elite who despised Him. But once He was gone, they would no longer have Him physically as their guide. They would need strength, comfort, and guidance far beyond their own ability. So, He promised them the Holy Spirit — a faithful Advocate — and assured them victory had already been won.

That same Advocate lives within every believer today. Jesus knew we would also need the Holy Spirit to guide, protect, and empower us to do far more than we could ever imagine. He did not leave us to face the world on our own. The Spirit guides and strengthens us every day. When we anchor our lives in His truth, no storm can ever uproot what He has already secured.

A Prayer to End

Dear Jesus, thank You for speaking peace into the hearts of Your disciples, even as You faced the reality of the cross. You saw their collective fear and gently gave them hope, truth, and encouragement. Thank You for sending us the Holy Spirit to comfort, guide, and remind us to live a life that honors and glorifies You. When the news of the day seems heavy or uncertain, help us take heart and remember, You have already overcome the world. Help us not waste time on circumstances we cannot control, and teach us to rest in Your presence. Amen.

Bible References

John 14 — Jesus promises the Holy Spirit and comforts His disciples
John 15 — The vine and the branches; love and obedience
John 16 — Warning of persecution, promise of joy, and victory over the world

Pause & Reflect — Mission

Bold Voice … Go!

Following Jesus was never meant to be a private experience. From the beginning, He called His followers to carry what they had received into the world around them. Not all were teachers or leaders, but all were witnesses. Jesus knew His disciples would feel unprepared, uncertain, and even afraid, yet He still sent them. He promised they would not go alone.

Boldness does not mean having all the answers or speaking perfectly. It means being willing to show up and trust God to work through us. Jesus understood fear would try to silence His followers, so He promised the help they would need. The Holy Spirit would guide their words, strengthen their hearts, and give them courage when their own confidence fell short.

When we live out our faith with humility and love, God uses our obedience to reach others. Sometimes that mission looks like speaking truth. Other times it looks like serving quietly, showing compassion, or standing firm in moments that test our faith. We may not always feel ready, but when God calls us to go, He also provides what we need along the way.

Memory Verse

"You will receive power when the Holy Spirit comes on you; and you will be my witnesses." — Acts 1:8

Questions to Consider

What areas of our lives might God be inviting us to live out our faith more boldly?

What fears or hesitations are keeping us from speaking to others about Jesus Christ?

A Prayer to End

Dear Jesus, thank You for trusting us to be part of Your work in the world. When we feel unsure or afraid, remind us that we do not go on our own. Fill us with Your Spirit, guide our words, and help us live in a way that reflects Your love and truth. Give us the courage to go where You lead and the faith to trust You every step of the way. Amen.

In the Year of Our Lord, ~AD 33

The Betrayal in the Garden

Jesus Withdraws to Pray in the Garden

After sharing words of encouragement and a promise of an Advocate or Helper, Jesus and His disciples left the city and made their way to the Kidron Valley. They came to a place called the Garden of Gethsemane, near the base of the Mount of Olives.

Jesus visited this area many times before to be alone with His Father. It was a peaceful place where He spent quiet time in prayer and reflected on the journey ahead. But this night was different. He told some of His disciples, "Sit here while I go over there and pray" (Matthew 26:36). Then He asked Peter, James, and John to come with Him. As they stepped away from the group, sorrow began to press upon Jesus and weigh Him down.

"My soul is overwhelmed with sorrow to the point of death," He said to them. "Stay here and keep watch with me" (Matthew 26:38). Then Jesus walked away from the disciples who were with Him, knelt down, and began to pour out His heart to the Father.

A Sorrowful Prayer, Disciples Can't Stay Awake

Jesus prayed with clarity and sorrow in the stillness of the night. "Abba, Father," He said, "everything is possible for You. Take this cup from me. Yet not what I will, but what you will" (Mark 14:36).

This prayer came from a place of deep struggle. His voice trembled. His whole mind, body, and soul wrestled with the weight of what lay ahead. The Book of Luke tells us "being in anguish, he prayed more earnestly, and his sweat was like drops of blood falling to the ground" (Luke 22:44). Jesus' sorrow wasn't normal; His agony was so great it came through His skin.

An angel descended from heaven and strengthened Him (Luke 22:43), but He still had to carry this burden alone. After He prayed, He returned to His disciples and found them fast asleep. "Couldn't you men keep watch with me for one hour?" He asked (Matthew 26:40). Then, Jesus left to pray again, and He came back the second time. His disciples were asleep once again.

He left a total of three times to pray, surrendering His life to His Father each time. After He prayed the last time, He rose to His feet and said, "The hour has come. Look, the Son of Man is delivered into the hands of sinners" (Mark 14:41).

Betrayed by a Kiss

Suddenly, the sound of footsteps marching in unison interrupted the peace of the night. A group of men in full body armor carrying torches, clubs, and swords entered the garden. Roman soldiers stood at the side of the Temple guards; the chief priests sent all of them to arrest Jesus. Leading the charge was someone Jesus and His disciples knew well: Judas Iscariot.

Judas had arranged a special signal: "The one I kiss is the man; arrest him" (Matthew 26:48). He approached Jesus and said, "Greetings, Rabbi!" and kissed him. Jesus calmly replied to Judas, "Do what you came for, friend" (Matthew 26:50).

The guards quickly seized Jesus. As they escorted Him out of the garden, Peter tried to defend Him. He drew his sword, swung it at one of the high priest's servants, and cut off his ear. But Jesus stepped in and stopped him, "Put your sword back in its place … Do you think I cannot call on my Father, and He will at once put at my disposal more than twelve legions of angels?" (Matthew 26:52–53).

But Jesus didn't call on His Father's angels to help. Instead, He surrendered, knowing this had to happen. "But how then would the Scriptures be fulfilled that say it must happen in this way?" (Matthew 26:54).

Everyone Deserts Him

Just as Jesus foretold, His disciples, scared and overwhelmed, ran away. The guards tied Him up and escorted Him back into the city to face the chief priests. The garden that had once been filled with peace and rest was now the place where the Lamb of God was handed over to die.

Why This Story Matters

In the Garden of Gethsemane, we experience a side of Jesus we rarely talk about — His anguish. He not only prepared for His death but also prepared to carry the sin of the entire world. He couldn't do this by Himself.

This moment shows us that when we are overwhelmed, real power comes when we take a knee and give our cares to God. We don't have to push through on our own.

This story also reminds us how easy it is to "fall asleep" in our faith. Jesus asked His disciples to stay alert, but exhaustion overtook them. Jesus responded differently. Though weary, He turned to His Father for strength and clarity, while the disciples allowed their weariness to pull them away from prayer.

Even when faced with betrayal and injustice, Jesus showed grace and restraint. He was strong and stayed true to the plan His Father had given Him. When the time for His arrest came, He went willingly, so we could receive the gift of eternal life with God.

A Prayer to End

Dear Jesus, thank You for sharing with us what true courage looks like. In the Garden of Gethsemane, You felt the weight of the world on Your shoulders, but instead of turning and running the other way, You chose to stay and obey. When betrayal came Your way, You didn't fight back but trusted the Father's will, even when it cost You everything. Help us stay awake in our faith, keeping watch and remaining prayerful when it's hard, so we don't miss out on what You're doing around us. Amen.

Bible References

Matthew 26 — Jesus prays in Gethsemane; the disciples fall asleep; Judas betrays Jesus; Jesus is arrested

Mark 14 — Jesus' sorrowful prayer; His arrest in the garden

Luke 22 — Jesus' anguish; an angel strengthens Him; betrayal and arrest in Gethsemane

In the Year of Our Lord, ~AD 33

The Trial of an Innocent King

Jesus Arrested

The soldiers bound and dragged Jesus from the Garden of Gethsemane and led Him to the high priest's house. The disciples feared for their lives and fled when they saw this. But Peter followed Jesus at a distance, staying just close enough to observe what was unfolding.

Inside the house, the Jewish religious leaders — the Pharisees, Sadducees, and chief priests — waited for Jesus to arrive. They had planned to kill Him for a long time, but they didn't have the power to execute anyone under Roman law (John 18:31). Only a Roman governor could have someone executed. So, they had to move forward with their plan carefully.

False Charges Made in the Dark

At the home of Caiaphas, the high priest, they held a secret trial in the middle of the night, an illegal act by their own rules. They brought in false witnesses to discredit Jesus, but their testimonies did not agree with each other (Mark 14:56). Some stated that He threatened to destroy the Temple. Others lied and twisted His words.

Caiaphas grew impatient with the progress of the trial, so He stood up and asked, "Are you the Messiah, the Son of the Blessed One?" (Mark 14:61). Jesus replied, "I am … and you will see the Son of Man sitting at the right hand of the Mighty One and coming on the clouds of heaven" (Mark 14:62).

The high priest tore his robe off his chest when he heard Jesus' reply and cried, "Blasphemy!" The council immediately sentenced Him to death, and those in attendance spat on Him and beat Him. But since they could not kill Jesus on their own, they prepared to hand Him over to the Romans to do their dirty work for them.

Peter Denies Jesus

Peter lingered nearby as Jesus stood trial, even though he tried to stay hidden. A servant girl recognized him as she sat by the fire. "You also were with Jesus of Galilee," she said. Peter adamantly denied it. "I don't know what you're talking about." Two more times, people accused him of being one of Jesus' disciples, and each time Peter denied knowing Him. After he denied Jesus the third time, the rooster crowed, just as Jesus had predicted. Peter ran outside and wept bitterly (Matthew 26:69–75).

Jesus Stands Before Pilate and King Herod

Early the next day, the religious leaders took Jesus to Pontius Pilate, the Roman governor. They couldn't accuse Him of blasphemy — claiming He was the Son of God — because a Roman governor would not consider that a crime. So, they twisted Jesus' words and said He claimed to be the King of the Jews and forbade paying taxes to Caesar (Luke 23:2). Both charges were considered treason under Roman law.

Pilate asked Jesus, "Are you the King of the Jews?" And Jesus responded, "You have said so" (Luke 23:3). Still, Pilate couldn't find a legitimate charge to pin on Him. So, to avoid involvement in the growing controversy, Pilate sent Jesus to King Herod, since Jesus was from Galilee and Herod had authority over that region. But Jesus refused to speak to Herod. Out of spite, Herod publicly mocked Jesus' claim to be King by dressing Him in a fancy robe; then, he sent Him back to Pilate for judgment.

Barabbas Freed and Jesus Condemned

Pilate desperately wanted to set Jesus free, but he needed the crowd's agreement. So, in keeping with Passover tradition, he gave the people a choice to decide which prisoner to set free — Jesus or Barabbas, a well-known criminal. "Which one do you want me to release to you?" Pilate asked (Matthew 27:17). The religious elders encouraged the crowd to choose Barabbas. And they did.

"What shall I do, then, with Jesus?" Pilate asked. "Crucify Him!" the crowd shouted (Matthew 27:22).

Pilate felt uneasy about their decision. He called for a bowl of water and washed his hands before the crowd. "I am innocent of this man's blood," he said. "It is your responsibility!" (Matthew 27:24). Then Pilate gave Jesus over to the Roman guards to be crucified.

Crown of Thorns

The Roman soldiers took Jesus to a jail cell, took off His clothes, and placed a scarlet robe over His shoulders. They made a crown of thorns and pressed it into His head, causing his head to bleed. They mocked Him, kneeled before Him, and said, "Hail, king of the Jews!" (Matthew 27:29). Then they struck Him again and led Him away.

Why This Story Matters

This was the most unjust trial in human history. Everyone present knew Jesus was completely innocent. The religious leaders lied and manipulated the crowd. Pilate avoided responsibility. Herod mocked Jesus but didn't want His death on his hands. And Peter, though loyal to Jesus, denied Him three times out of fear.

Still, Jesus didn't try to run away. He didn't argue. He didn't call on a higher power to fight this fight on His behalf. He stood silent and surrendered Himself for our sakes; He knew this was the only path to our salvation and the only way back to the Father.

This story reminds us that Jesus came into a broken world, surrounded by a violent crowd, and received an undeserved sentence. He faced and conquered the greatest injustice so all our sins would be forgiven, and we could walk into new life — restored, redeemed, and made complete in Him.

A Prayer to End

Dear Jesus, You could have called on angels at any time to help You, or even walked away, but You didn't. Thank You for standing strong and obedient in the face of false accusations, mockery, and physical abuse. You carried it all on our behalf so we could be saved and given new life, and for that we praise You. In our moments of weakness and fear, help us remain faithful to who You are and to the truth You have shown us, so that we may share Your story with those around us. Amen.

Bible References

John 18 — Jesus is arrested and taken before the high priest and Pilate

Mark 14 — False witnesses accuse Jesus; Jesus before Caiaphas; Peter denies Him

Matthew 26–27 — Peter denies Jesus; Jesus before Pilate; Barabbas released; Jesus mocked and condemned

Luke 23 — Jesus before Pilate and King Herod

In the Year of Our Lord, ~AD 33

The Crucifixion of Jesus

The Road to the Cross

Word spread quickly throughout Jerusalem: Jesus of Nazareth was sentenced to die. Just days earlier, the people cheered as He rode into the city, waving palm branches in the air and calling Him King. But now, many of those same people lined the streets for a far more somber reason, watching a beaten and exhausted Jesus be paraded before them as He made His way toward the cross.

The Roman guards led Jesus through the streets, making Him carry His own crossbeam, a heavy piece of rough wood placed across the middle of His swollen back (John 19:17). He had been beaten earlier in the day, and now a crown of thorns was put on top of His head again. Blood dripped from His forehead with every step He took.

As they escorted Jesus to a hill called Golgotha, also known as the Place of the Skull, He fell beneath the crossbeam's weight. He was too weak to keep going. So, the soldiers grabbed a man from among the crowd, Simon of Cyrene, and made him carry the cross. He walked a few steps behind Jesus (Luke 23:26).

Carrying the cross in the streets was meant to publicly humiliate and shame Jesus. People shouted, spat, and threw things as He walked past them. Some in the crowd wept. But Jesus kept going. Each step drew Him closer to the moment that would change the world.

The Crucifixion

Once He arrived at Golgotha, Jesus was nailed to the cross. His hands and feet were pierced to the wood. Two criminals were on each side of Him, both awaiting execution for their crimes. Above Jesus' head, the Roman soldiers attached a sign that read, "Jesus of Nazareth, the King of the Jews" (John 19:19). The religious elite didn't like it. "Do not write 'The King of the Jews,'" they told Pilate. But Pilate answered, "What I have written, I have written" (John 19:21–22).

As Jesus hung on the cross, the soldiers in charge of the crucifixion cast lots to decide who would get His tunic (John 19:23–24). Casting lots was a form of gambling by rolling dice.

It was common among Roman soldiers to divide the belongings of those they crucified so they could sell the items back to the deceased person's family.

Two Criminals, Two Hearts

One of the criminals made fun of Jesus in the same way the crowd mocked Him. "Aren't you the Messiah?" he sneered. "Save yourself, and us!" The other man sternly corrected him: "Don't you fear God? … We are punished justly … but this man has done nothing wrong." Then he turned and pleaded with Jesus, "Jesus, remember me when you come into your kingdom." Jesus looked at him with empathy and said, "Truly I tell you, today you will be with me in paradise" (Luke 23:39–43).

Mocked and Thirsty

The religious leaders and passersby laughed at Jesus. "You who are going to destroy the temple and build it in three days, save yourself! Come down from the cross, if you are the Son of God!" (Matthew 27:40). But Jesus didn't come down; He remained on the cross. Later, Jesus said, "I am thirsty" (John 19:28). So, the soldiers lifted a sponge soaked in wine vinegar to His mouth. Roman soldiers drank wine vinegar — leftover wine mixed with vinegar — to stay hydrated during hot days in the field.

After wetting his lips, Jesus cried out in a loud voice, "Father, forgive them, for they do not know what they are doing" (Luke 23:34). Eventually, he spoke His final words: "It is finished. Father, into your hands I commit my spirit" (John 19:30; Luke 23:46). With that, Jesus took His last breath.

The Curtain Torn and the Sky Darkened

At the same time, an earthquake shook the land. Rocks split in two, and tombs opened wide. The sky went dark from noon until three in the afternoon, now groaning with sorrow (Matthew 27:45, 51–52).

Inside the Temple, the thick curtain that separated the Most Holy Place from those in attendance suddenly tore into two pieces from top to bottom (Matthew 27:51). The heavy barrier had long represented the separation between mankind's sinful nature and God's holiness. It was believed that the innermost room of the Temple, called the Most Holy Place, was where God's presence resided. The tearing of the curtain symbolized something powerful: through Jesus' death, the way back to God was now open to all mankind.

When a Roman soldier at the foot of the cross saw all that happened, he whispered what many were now thinking, "Surely this man was the Son of God!" (Mark 15:39).

Why This Story Matters

After Jesus' death, the chief priests witnessed undeniable signs from heaven. Darkness covered the sky in the middle of the day. The temple curtain was torn in two, and the earth shook beneath their feet. These were direct acts of God, confirming the Son of God had just been killed on a cross, fulfilling the very Scriptures they claimed to uphold. The prophet Isaiah spoke of this moment nearly seven hundred years before Jesus' death:

"But he was pierced for our transgressions, he was crushed for our iniquities; the punishment that brought us peace was on him, and by his wounds we are healed" (Isaiah 53:5).

Jesus carried the weight of the cross no one else could bear. He offered forgiveness even as people insulted and mocked Him. Through His sacrifice, He tore down the barriers of religion and opened the way for us to have a direct relationship with the Father.

As Jesus suffered on the cross, one of the criminals crucified beside Him asked to be remembered when Jesus came into His Kingdom. This man was guilty, being punished for serious crimes, yet in his final moments, he turned to Jesus in faith, asking for forgiveness. And with love and grace, Jesus welcomed him.

How beautiful that it's never too late for anyone to turn to Him. Jesus completed the work that made forgiveness possible for the entire world.

A Prayer to End

Dear Jesus, thank You for the strength and courage You displayed by accepting pain, shame, and death You did not deserve. When You breathed Your last breath, You paved a way for us to return home. Help us never forget the sacrifice You made to give us eternal life with God. We praise Your holy name, Jesus, for loving us all the way to the cross. Amen.

Bible References

Luke 23 — Simon of Cyrene carries the cross; criminals crucified beside Jesus; Jesus promises paradise

John 19 — Jesus carries the crossbeam and is crucified; soldiers cast lots; Jesus declares "It is finished."

Matthew 27 — Jesus is mocked; darkness covers the land; the Temple curtain tears

Mark 15 — Roman centurion declares Jesus the Son of God

Isaiah 53 — Jesus pierced for our transgressions

In the Year of Our Lord, ~AD 33

The Burial of Jesus and the Guard at the Tomb

When Faith Steps Forward

Sadness filled the air when Jesus took His last breath. The earth shook. Rocks split open. The great curtain in the Temple split in two. People left the hill at Golgotha in silence, many not knowing how to comprehend what they had just witnessed.

But one man stayed behind. His name was Joseph of Arimathea, and he stood quietly near the cross. He was a rich, respected member of the Jewish ruling elite, the Sanhedrin. He didn't agree with the decision to execute Jesus. Joseph was a follower of Jesus, but he kept his loyalty private, fearful of what might happen to him if his belief in Jesus went public. But this changed when he saw Jesus pass away; he felt compelled to step forward.

Joseph's Brave Request

Joseph asked Pontius Pilate for permission to recover Jesus' body (Matthew 27:58). It was a courageous request, one that could expose his belief in the Man the council had just executed. But Joseph was determined, his faith now greater than his fear.

Pilate was surprised to learn Jesus had passed away so quickly. He confirmed His death with a centurion, a Roman soldier who commanded one hundred troops, and then gave Joseph permission to take his body (Mark 15:44–45).

Joseph took Jesus down from the cross carefully, and Nicodemus, another secret believer who once visited Jesus in the middle of the night, joined him. Together, they brought a mixture of myrrh and aloes, weighing about seventy-five pounds, to honor Jesus and prepare His body for burial (John 19:39). This was a costly act, fit for a king.

Based on Jewish custom, those who cared for Jesus' body wrapped it in clean linen cloths and gently anointed it with a mixture of spices (Luke 23:56). Mary Magdalene, Mary the mother of James, and other women observed this sacred process closely. Though men typically led the burial, it was usually women, skilled in preparing bodies for rest, who ensured that those who passed away were honored and wrapped with tenderness.

In a nearby garden, Joseph gave up a tomb he had purchased so Jesus would have a peaceful burial site. Jesus' body was gently placed inside, and a large stone was rolled across the entrance. The women sat across from the tomb, grieving, while keeping a watchful eye on it (Matthew 27:60–61).

The Religious Leaders' Fear

The next day, after Jesus was crucified, the chief priests and Pharisees came to Pilate. This time, they didn't seek a death sentence; they sought control. "Sir," they said, "we remember that while he was still alive that deceiver said, 'After three days I will rise again'" (Matthew 27:63).

They no longer worried about Jesus Himself but were concerned His story would live on after He was gone. They were convinced His disciples would steal His body at night and claim Jesus had risen. If His followers pulled off this plan, then this deception would be worse than the first — convincing people Jesus was the Son of God.

The Pharisees requested that Pilate secure Jesus' tomb, to seal the entryway with a stone, and post guards outside. Pilate agreed. "Take a guard," he said. "Go, make the tomb as secure as you know how." So, the tomb was sealed with a stone, and Roman soldiers guarded it day and night (Matthew 27:65–66).

The religious elite found it hard to believe Jesus could rise from the dead, so they convinced themselves that a stone and a few guards would be enough to stop Him. What they did not realize was that God had already set His plan in motion, and no stone or soldier could stand in the way.

Why This Story Matters

The religious leaders couldn't bring themselves to accept that the supernatural events they had just witnessed pointed to their failure to recognize Jesus for who He truly was. Instead of turning to God in repentance, their hearts grew cold to what He had revealed. They doubled down, approaching Pilate in an attempt to silence the very message Jesus preached — that He would rise again, proving He truly was the Son of God.

Pride kept many from acknowledging what their hearts already knew, but not everyone responded the same way.

Joseph and Nicodemus had long known Jesus was different, yet they followed Him from a distance, hesitant to step fully into the light. It was only after His unjust death, with broken hearts, that they finally stepped forward in boldness to honor the living God. This story reminds us that faith often shows itself through quiet acts of courage, especially when the cost is high and the future uncertain.

As our faith grows, so does our courage to speak about our Lord and Savior. The world will try to silence us, just as the religious elite tried to silence the message of Jesus' resurrection. But we must stand firm in His truth, sharing His life and His story with a world desperate for hope, trusting that God's story through us is only beginning.

For the Bible says, "The light shines in the darkness, and the darkness has not overcome it" (John 1:5).

A Prayer to End

Dear Jesus, thank You for the courage You give to those who choose to follow You. When we feel afraid to speak about our faith or worry about how others might see us, remind us we are never alone. Fill us with bravery and confidence to speak truth with love, even when it feels uncomfortable. Help us care more about honoring You than being accepted by others, and give us the strength to stand firm in who You have called us to be. Amen.

Bible References

Matthew 27 — Joseph asks for Jesus' body; the tomb is sealed and guarded
Mark 15 — Pilate confirms Jesus' death; Joseph buries Jesus
John 19 — Nicodemus brings spices; Jesus' body prepared for burial
Luke 23 — Women witness the burial and prepare spices
John 1 — Darkness shall not overcome the light

Easter Sunday — Jesus Is Risen

When Hope Seemed Lost

It was early Sunday morning, just after the Sabbath, and the streets of Jerusalem were once again quiet. Since Friday, Jesus' followers had been devastated by the news of His death. The Man they followed and believed to be the Messiah, the Son of God, was taken from them. Their Teacher, their hope, died on a cross and was now buried in a tomb and no longer with them.

Most of the disciples went into hiding. They stayed indoors and never left their homes, afraid they'd be noticed by the Jewish leaders or Roman authorities. They lived in fear, knowing they could be murdered just like Jesus. No one knew what they should do next. The only thing they knew for sure was that they were broken by Jesus' death on the cross.

The Women at the Tomb

Early the next morning, while it was still dark outside, two faithful women walked toward Jesus' tomb: Mary Magdalene and Mary, the mother of James. These women supported Jesus during His life and now, in His death. With faithful hearts full of love and sorrow, they carried spices and perfumes to anoint His body and show Him one last act of honor (Luke 24:1).

As they approached His tomb, an earthquake suddenly shook the ground and caused them to stumble. Then, right before their eyes, an angel of the Lord appeared. He rolled away the massive stone that enclosed Jesus' tomb and sat on it. The angel shone like the sun, and his clothes were made of the purest white linen. The Roman soldiers were so scared that they immediately collapsed to the ground in fear (Matthew 28:2–4).

The Angel's Message

The angel turned, looked at the women, and said in a gentle voice, "Do not be afraid, for I know that you are looking for Jesus, who was crucified. He is not here; he has risen, just as he said. Come and see the place where he lay" (Matthew 28:5–6).

The two Marys cautiously stepped forward, still shaking with fear, and looked into the tomb. The tomb was empty just as the angel had said. The place where Jesus' body once lay was now bare, except for His burial cloths. Jesus had risen just as He had promised.

The angel then said, "Go quickly and tell his disciples: 'He has risen from the dead and is going ahead of you into Galilee. There you will see him'" (Matthew 28:7).

A Joyful Encounter

The women rejoiced over what they had just witnessed and heard, and they rushed back to tell the others. Along the way, something even more amazing happened: Jesus appeared to them both. He greeted them warmly, and they immediately dropped to their knees, reaching out to touch His feet, and began to worship Him (Matthew 28:8–9).

Jesus said gently, "Do not be afraid. Go and tell my brothers to go to Galilee; there they will see me" (Matthew 28:10).

Imagine the pure joy they must have felt when they saw Him. Excitement, wonder, and hope quickly replaced the sadness they had carried for three days.

The Guards' Report

The soldiers who guarded Jesus' tomb collapsed in fear when the earth trembled, and He rose from the grave. But they were awake now and fled the scene. They made their way back to the chief priests' residences and told them everything. The religious leaders were troubled by what they heard. Instead of believing Jesus was the long-awaited Savior and Messiah, they tried to contain the situation. They were determined to protect their authority and ensure no one else heard about the miracle. So, they paid the soldiers a large sum of silver coins and ordered them to lie about what they saw.

As part of the deal, the guards made up this story: A group of men, led by Jesus' disciples, took them by surprise, overpowered them, rolled away the stone, and took Jesus' body (Matthew 28:11–15).

A New Dawn

Back in town, the disciples continued to hide in their homes, fearing for their lives. They had no idea that during this eventful morning, two faithful women had received a message that would soon change the world: Jesus was alive!

Why This Story Matters

Early Sunday morning, the two Marys made their way to the tomb. Even in their grief, they chose to draw near to Jesus once more, unaware that God had already gone before them. When they arrived, an angel appeared and announced that Jesus was no longer there. The stone had been rolled away, not to let Jesus out, but to let them see the tomb was empty. The angel invited them to believe what had taken place and to remember Jesus' words, that He would rise again.

Because the two Marys came with hearts open in faith, they were able to hear and receive the angel's message. They did not dismiss it or turn away in fear. Instead, they believed. And they were not only entrusted with the news of the resurrection, but also with the responsibility to share it with others.

This story reminds us God is always faithful to His promises. He moves first. He prepares the way. And when we respond in faith, we are able to see what He has already done. The resurrection was not stopped by human power, fear, or force. Jesus did exactly what He said He would do, just as Scripture foretold. He came. He was rejected. He was crucified. And on the third day, He rose again.

The empty tomb opened the way for new life for all who believe. Just as the two Marys arrived in grief but left with joy and purpose, we too are invited to trust God in our darkest moments and to share the hope we have been given. Jesus is alive.

A Prayer to End

Dear Jesus, when life feels uncertain, fill us with the joy that comes from knowing the tomb is still empty, and You are alive. Give us the faith the two Marys had, a faith that continues forward, even when things look lost or hopeless. Thank You for the Good News that comes through knowing You — death has been defeated, and our lives have been restored. Amen.

Bible References

Matthew 28 — Mary Magdalene and the other Mary visit the tomb; the angel announces Jesus has risen

Luke 24 — The two Marys walk to Jesus' tomb to anoint His body

Eastertide

The Resurrection was not the end. In the days that followed, Jesus appeared to His followers, confirming the truth of the Scriptures and strengthening their faith.

These readings recount the moments between Jesus' resurrection and His ascension into heaven.

This sacred season is often called Eastertide, the Easter Season, or the Paschal Season. Traditionally, it spans fifty days, from the Resurrection to Pentecost, the moment when the Holy Spirit fully came upon the disciples as they waited in the upper room, just as Jesus had promised. The readings in this section focus on the forty days when Jesus appeared to His disciples before ascending into heaven.

In the Year of Our Lord, ~AD 33

The Road to Emmaus — Hopeful Hearts

A Journey Begins in Sadness

The same day Jesus rose from the dead, two of His followers left town and made their way to a small town called Emmaus, about seven miles away from Jerusalem (Luke 24:13). One of His followers was named Cleopas (Luke 24:18); the other follower's name is not mentioned in Scripture, but they were both close to Jesus and His disciples.

They walked slowly, recounting the amazing circumstances that had transpired over the last couple of days. They weren't sure what to believe, the reports that He was dead or the reports that He was alive, but they still hoped He was the One to redeem Israel (Luke 24:21). Nothing made sense to them anymore now that Jesus was gone.

A Stranger Joins Them on the Road

As Cleopas and his friend continued their journey, a man came alongside them and walked with them. Somehow, neither of the friends recognized Him; it was Jesus Himself (Luke 24:15–16). Scripture explains they were kept from seeing Him because God had a specific purpose for this encounter.

Jesus asked, "What are you discussing together as you walk along?" (Luke 24:17).

Surprised by the man's question, the two friends stopped, their faces full of despair (Luke 24:17). Cleopas replied, "Are you the only one visiting Jerusalem who does not know the things that have happened there in these days?" (Luke 24:18).

"What things?" Jesus asked (Luke 24:19).

They began to share Jesus' story, not realizing they were actually speaking with Him. They spoke of Jesus of Nazareth, a prophet with authority who performed many miracles, but was handed over to Pontius Pilate to be crucified (Luke 24:19–20). "We had hoped that he was the one who was going to redeem Israel," they said. (Luke 24:21). They also mentioned how some women, who also followed Jesus, went to the tomb early that morning, found it empty, and claimed angels told them He was alive. But the disciples had not seen Him alive yet (Luke 24:22–24).

The Truth Comes to Light

Jesus listened, then said, "How foolish you are, and how slow to believe all that the prophets have spoken!" (Luke 24:25). As they continued walking, Jesus began explaining the Scriptures to them, starting with Moses and all of the Prophets, and showing them how the Scriptures pointed to the Messiah (Luke 24:27). He explained how the Christ had to suffer these things before entering His glory (Luke 24:26).

Eyes Opened at the Table

By the time they reached Emmaus, evening had come, and the day was almost over. Jesus was in the middle of saying goodbye to Cleopas and his friend, but they urged Him, "Stay with us, for it is nearly evening; the day is almost over" (Luke 24:28–29). So, He accepted their invitation to stay.

While they gathered at the table, Jesus took some bread, gave thanks and prayed, broke it, and began to give it to them. Suddenly, their eyes were opened, and they recognized Him, but before they could say anything, He disappeared from their sight (Luke 24:30–31).

They looked at one another in disbelief and said, "Were not our hearts burning within us while He talked with us on the road and opened the Scriptures to us?" (Luke 24:32). The deep sorrow they had been carrying was gone. They now knew the women's report was true. Jesus had risen!

Back to Jerusalem with Joy

Cleopas and his traveling companion were so excited, they couldn't sit still; they had to tell the others what they had witnessed. Even though it was late, they hurried back seven miles to Jerusalem (Luke 24:33).

Once there, they found the disciples sitting together and were greeted with wonderful news themselves before they could get a word out: "It is true! The Lord has risen and has appeared to Simon!" (Luke 24:34).

The two disciples were shocked when they realized Jesus had appeared to Peter, too.

Then Cleopas and his friend explained their own encounter with Jesus. How He had walked alongside them on the road and taught them Scripture, and how they finally recognized Him when He broke the bread during supper (Luke 24:35). Understanding and joy now prevailed over the disciples' initial confusion and despair, and everyone was filled with hope.

Why This Story Matters

Right before His arrest, Jesus prepared His disciples for life without His physical presence. Time was short, yet He continued to teach, urging them to carry on the work He had begun.

The two disciples on the road to Emmaus remembered every detail of Jesus' life — His travels, His miracles, even His death. They remembered the Man, but they had lost sight of the mission. Jesus saw their weakness and knew they needed renewed hope. But before revealing Himself to them, He once again stepped into the role of a teacher.

As they walked together, Jesus took them back to the Scriptures. He did more than simply recite words; He helped them understand how His ministry, rejection, judgment, crucifixion, and resurrection unfolded exactly as God had promised. These were not accidents or failures but fulfilled prophecies. And through it all, He reminded them that their calling was to carry this Good News into a broken world.

This story reminds us that real faith grows not only through miracles but through walking with Jesus day by day. Even when we feel confused or lost, He walks beside us. He listens, He teaches, and He patiently reminds us of the truth. And at just the right moment, He opens our eyes to see He has been with us all along, calling us to something greater than we ever imagined.

A Prayer to End

Dear Jesus, thank You for walking by our side, even when we feel alone, lost, or discouraged. Open our hearts, just as You opened the Scriptures to the two men traveling on the road to Emmaus. Give us wisdom to walk in Your presence daily. And, just as Cleopas welcomed You without recognizing who You were, help us welcome others with the same kindness, respect, and hospitality. Amen.

Bible References

Luke 24 — The road to Emmaus; Jesus explains the Scriptures and reveals Himself in Emmaus

In the Year of Our Lord, ~AD 33

Jesus Appears to the Ten Disciples

Whispers in Jerusalem

Evening spread across Jerusalem's busy stone streets, and the tension in the city was thick. Whispers that Jesus' tomb was empty moved through the city faster than the authorities could contain them. Some dismissed the reports, others argued over explanations, but one message refused to be silenced: Jesus has risen.

Behind Locked Doors

Inside an upper room, Jesus' disciples gathered behind locked doors, not because they hadn't heard anything, but because they had heard too much. The two Marys returned from the tomb, declaring that an angel had spoken. Cleopas and his friend rushed back from Emmaus, insisting they had walked with Jesus Himself. Peter, too, claimed to see Him alive. And yet fear still gripped their hearts. The trauma of the crucifixion was fresh, and the threat of arrest felt real.

They wanted to believe. Hope flickered. But the image of the cross had not yet faded, and now faith wrestled with fear. Could it possibly be true? Could Jesus really be alive, just as He had promised?

Then, without a knock, without warning, without the door opening, Jesus appeared among them. His first words to them? "Peace be with you!" (John 20:19).

The disciples were shocked. As they struggled to get their bearings, Jesus stretched out His arms to show them His hands, and then He showed them His side. The piercings from the nails and the spear were still visible on His body (John 20:20). Then they knew. This wasn't a vision. Jesus was alive, standing right there in the room!

Peace Replaces Fear

Still stunned, the disciples watched as Jesus asked for something to eat. They gave Him a piece of broiled fish, and He ate it in front of them with a thankful heart, just as He had done so many times before (Luke 24:41–43).

Then Jesus opened their minds to understand the Scriptures (Luke 24:45). He reminded them of everything He had taught them, how the law of Moses, the Prophets, and the Psalms all pointed to this moment. The Messiah had to suffer, die, and rise again on the third day (Luke 24:44–46).

His victory did not come by sword or army, but through service, sacrifice, and resurrection. His mission was not to overthrow the Romans but to conquer death and overcome the world. As this reality sank in for the disciples, their fear turned into joy and wonder; their Lord had returned just as He foretold.

Sent with the Spirit

Now, the work would continue through them. "You are witnesses of these things," Jesus said (Luke 24:48). "Repentance for the forgiveness of sins will be preached in [my] name to all nations, beginning at Jerusalem" (Luke 24:47). Then He looked at them with great love and said, "As the Father has sent me, I am sending you" (John 20:21).

Jesus stepped closer, exhaled, and said, "Receive the Holy Spirit" (John 20:22). This was not the full outpouring of the Spirit; that sacred moment would come later at Pentecost. Pentecost was the time when God sent the Holy Spirit to dwell within believers, giving them a faithful guide to help them walk with the Lord, understand His truth, and live out their faith with courage and confidence.

What Jesus offered here was preparation for what was yet to come. He told them what they needed to do, and He gave them assurance they would not face it alone. The Advocate was on the way.

Just as quickly as Jesus appeared to them, He was gone, but His peace remained in the room, a room that had once been filled with emptiness and sorrow. The disciples looked at one another, hopeful yet speechless. For the first time in days, they felt joy. They knew Jesus' Spirit was still with them.

One Disciple Missing

One of the disciples missed this special moment with Jesus. Thomas, also called Didymus, wasn't with the other disciples when Jesus appeared (John 20:24). Maybe he had gone to get food for the group or found a quiet place in the garden to pray. Whatever the reason, he wasn't prepared for what awaited him.

"We have seen the Lord!" they all shouted when Thomas joined them (John 20:25).

But he couldn't believe it. He shook his head and said quietly, "Unless I see the nail marks in His hands and put my finger where the nails were, and put my hand into His side, I will not believe" (John 20:25). No one could convince him.

Although a week went by before Jesus appeared again, nothing could keep Him away from those He loved so deeply.

Why This Story Matters

When the disciples were alone, gathered behind locked doors in fear and uncertainty, Jesus sought them out. He came to them with love and peace, not with judgment or frustration. He knew they struggled to believe, so He showed them His wounds to give them confidence that it was truly Him. In their brief time together, He reminded them of the truth found in Scripture, outlined their mission, and gave them the strength to carry it out.

How amazing it is that Jesus knew exactly what they needed, and precisely the moment they needed it. They were desperate for His presence and support more than ever, especially as they faced the reality of moving forward without Him physically by their side. Though the full outpouring of the Holy Spirit had not yet come, Jesus understood the seriousness of their condition. Without receiving a portion of the Spirit's power and peace, they might not have been ready to leave the upper room.

This story reminds us that Jesus meets us where we are. When fear and doubt overwhelm us, we are not alone. When we call on His name, the Spirit gives us strength to stand firm and move forward with hope and purpose.

A Prayer to End

Dear Jesus, thank You for always being near, even when we struggle to understand who You are or what our purpose is. In moments of doubt or confusion, be our comfort and strength. Surround us with mentors who can guide us in truth, pray over us, and teach us, just as you did for the disciples. Help us know and understand the mission You have given us, and clothe us with the courage to walk in it. Amen.

Bible References

John 20 — Jesus appears to His disciples in the locked room and shows them His wounds
Luke 24 — Jesus opens the disciples' minds and fills them with peace

In the Year of Our Lord, ~AD 33

Jesus Appears to a Doubting Thomas

A Disciple Who Asked Honest Questions

Thomas wasn't just a disciple who doubted. He was a brave man who deeply cared about truth and Jesus. He followed Him closely, paid attention whenever He taught, and didn't avoid tough challenges. One time when Jesus decided to return to Judea, even though it was dangerous, it was Thomas who bravely said, "Let us also go, that we may die with him" (John 11:16).

During the Last Supper, when Jesus spoke about leaving to prepare a place for His followers, it was Thomas who asked the honest question everyone was thinking, "Lord, we don't know where you are going, so how can we know the way?" (John 14:5). Thomas wasn't afraid to speak up. He didn't want to pretend; he truly wanted to understand and believe.

When Hope Was Hard to Hold

But after Jesus' crucifixion, everything changed. Thomas had placed all of his hope in Jesus, but that hope disappeared when His body was taken down from the cross. Like the other disciples, Thomas' world was turned upside down. Nothing made sense anymore. The man he believed was the Messiah had died.

So, when Thomas returned to the upper room where the other disciples were gathered, he couldn't believe they had seen the risen Jesus. That's when Thomas proclaimed he would not believe what the others had seen unless he saw Jesus himself and could place his hands on Jesus' wounds (John 20:25).

Thomas wasn't being stubborn. He was hurt. He couldn't understand why Jesus had appeared without him. He needed to know for himself that Jesus was truly alive.

Still Behind Locked Doors

Eight days passed, and the disciples were still gathered in the same house. Even though they had seen the risen Jesus, the doors remained locked (John 20:26). They were filled with fear, unsure if the religious leaders and Roman officials were hunting them. Seeing Jesus had renewed their faith, but they still didn't know what to do next.

Then, like before, Jesus suddenly appeared before them, standing in their presence even though no one let Him in. "Peace be with you!" (John 20:26). This time, He turned and approached Thomas directly. "Put your finger here," Jesus said. "See my hands. Reach out your hand and put it into my side. Stop doubting and believe" (John 20:27).

From Doubt to Worship

Jesus knew what was in Thomas' heart. He wasn't angry or disappointed that Thomas had doubted. With kindness, Jesus met him right where he was. Instead of pushing Thomas away, He invited him to come closer. But Thomas didn't need to reach out. The moment he saw Jesus, he knew the truth: Jesus was alive.

"My Lord and my God!" he said, falling to his knees, now in complete belief (John 20:28). Seeing Jesus in the flesh changed everything for Thomas. His doubt turned to worship, and his sadness turned to joy. His faith not only returned, but it also grew stronger.

Jesus left them with words meant for every believer, those then and those to come: "Because you have seen me, you have believed; blessed are those who have not seen and yet have believed" (John 20:29).

A Bold Faith That Traveled Far

According to early church history, Thomas went on to travel far from Jerusalem to share the Good News of Jesus. Historians believe he may have gone to India, preaching to people who had never heard the name of Jesus. He helped start churches, healed the sick, cared for the poor, and shared the story of the One who rose from the dead.

The same disciple who once said, "I won't believe unless I see," became a bold witness to people across the world.

Why This Story Matters

This story reminds us that even Jesus' closest followers had moments of doubt. Jesus didn't scold Thomas for needing proof; He met him with patience, peace, and understanding. Jesus knew Thomas genuinely wanted to believe, and when He showed Himself, Thomas' faith became unshakable.

Jesus used Thomas' struggle to prepare him for something greater. He knew Thomas would encounter others who wrestled with uncertainty as well. This moment in the upper room didn't weaken Thomas; it shaped him. His experience gave him compassion and strength to reach those who also needed to see before they could believe.

Jesus shapes our lives just as He shaped Thomas', turning our struggles into something good. All of us have a past. We have made wrong choices, we carry regret, or we hold on to things God never intended us to bear. But when we come to Jesus and surrender those burdens, He forgives us and lifts the weight from our shoulders.

Just like Thomas, the very things we overcome can become the testimony God uses to reach someone else on their own journey. He meets us in our uncertainty and transforms it into a faith strong enough to share.

A Prayer to End

Dear Jesus, thank You for being okay with us asking You tough questions and for continuing to meet us where we are. Sometimes, like Thomas, we also feel unsure about our purpose. Sometimes we want to believe, but we are afraid to put our hope in You. In those dark moments of uncertainty, help us draw closer to You. Bring us peace and transform our hearts as You did for those in the upper room. Give us the faith, courage, and strength to live out the purpose You have placed before us. Amen.

Bible References

John 11 — Thomas' courage on display
John 14 — Thomas asks Jesus a question
John 20 — Jesus appears to Thomas and strengthens his faith

In the Year of Our Lord, ~AD 33

Jesus Appears to the Disciples by the Sea

Walking Toward Obedience

When Mary Magdalene and the other women saw that Jesus was no longer in the tomb, an angel told them something important, "He has risen … go quickly and tell His disciples, 'He … is going ahead of you into Galilee. There you will see him'" (Matthew 28:6–7).

After hearing Mary's message and seeing Jesus, the disciples were no longer frozen with fear. Over the next few days, they left the safety they once found in the upper room and moved forward with courage and the direction they needed to begin the long walk to Galilee.

Galilee was more than seventy miles away from Jerusalem and would take them at least four days to travel there. But something in their hearts had changed. They no longer worried about who might see them or whether Roman officials followed them.

A Sea, an Unexpected Voice

It was midday by the time they reached the Sea of Galilee, and after some time settling in, Peter said, "I'm going out to fish," and six others went with him (John 21:2–3). The journey had been long and uncertain for the disciples, so they returned to something familiar, fishing. It was something they could do together to ease their minds. But after an entire night out on the water, they hadn't caught a thing.

The next day, as the sun began to rise, a man stood on the shore and called out to them, "Friends, haven't you any fish?" "No," they answered. He said, "Throw your net on the right side of the boat and you will find some" (John 21:5–6).

Early in His ministry, Jesus had called His first disciples by the sea. He had told them to "put out into deep water, and let down the nets for a catch" (Luke 5:4). At the time, they questioned His request, saying, "Master, we've worked hard all night and haven't caught anything" (Luke 5:5).

But this time was different. Maybe they were too tired to argue. Maybe they sensed something familiar about the man standing on the shore. Maybe Peter already knew it was Jesus. But this time, they didn't hesitate. They cast their net immediately.

Recognizing the Lord

The net was filled with fish the moment it hit the water, and the disciples struggled to pull it back into the boat. Even though it held 153 large fish, the net didn't break (John 21:11). Then John turned to Peter and said, "It is the Lord!" (John 21:7).

Peter didn't second-guess his decision. He put on his outer garment and leaped into the water, swimming to shore with all his strength. The other disciples followed him in the boat, dragging with them the heavy net full of fish (John 21:7–8).

Breakfast by the Fire

Jesus prepared a small fire along with fish and bread. He said, "Bring some of the fish you have just caught," and invited them to eat (John 21:10, 12).

They gathered quietly around the small fire. No one spoke up to ask who He was; they all knew. "This was now the third time Jesus appeared to his disciples after he was raised from the dead" (John 21:14). But this time around, their gathering was about restoring past relationships.

In the quietness of that morning, Jesus fed them not only with food, but also with His presence, peace, and friendship.

Why This Story Matters

The disciples had once been afraid, unsure, and scattered after Jesus' death, hiding in an upper room and paralyzed by grief. But after Jesus appeared to them, He gave them exactly what they needed: encouragement and a renewed sense of faith. With that assurance, they walked freely to Galilee, no longer bound by fear.

Jesus could sense the disciples were growing into the individuals He had always known they could become. They were no longer consumed by concerns of being captured or hesitant to live out their faith openly. Their purpose was becoming clearer, and their confidence more settled. Earlier in Jesus' ministry, the disciples had been sent out to heal and perform miracles, only to later falter when asked to trust Him again with a new task. But this moment was different.

When Jesus instructed them from the shore to cast their nets once more, the disciples did not question or hesitate. They simply obeyed. Their immediate response revealed a deeper trust, even before they recognized that it was Jesus speaking to them. The net, heavy with fish, yet unbroken, reminded them that the mission ahead would be fruitful, but not easy.

It would require strength, prayer, and faith. And still, Jesus would be with them every step of the way.

This story reminds us that faith grows through obedience. When we take small steps of trust, Jesus meets us there, guiding us and reminding us of our purpose. Even on days when we feel tired or unsure, His familiar voice still calls to us, inviting us to trust Him again and move forward with confidence.

A Prayer to End

Jesus, thank You for loving us so deeply. Thank You for being patient with us as we continue to learn and grow in our faith. As we do, help us look for the ways You are working in our lives. Guide us by Your loving presence in all we do. Give us confidence in Your plan and help us share Your story with those around us. When the things of this world try to distract us or pull us away, help us stay focused on what matters to You. Amen.

Bible References

Matthew 28 — The angel sends the women to tell the disciples to go to Galilee
John 21 — Jesus appears to His disciples by the Sea of Galilee
Luke 5 — Jesus calls His first disciples by the sea

In the Year of Our Lord, ~AD 33

When Grace Rebuilds What Shame Tore Down

The Failure That Haunted Him

Peter had always been brave. He was the first disciple to walk on water, the first to announce Jesus as the Messiah, and the one who promised he would never leave Jesus' side. But on the night of Jesus' arrest, fear dominated him when people asked him if he was a follower of Jesus. His lack of faith led Peter to do what he thought he'd never do: he denied Jesus three times. Then, after the rooster crowed, he remembered Jesus' words and wept bitterly (Luke 22:61–62).

Peter stayed with the other disciples behind a locked door in the days that followed. He had visited and seen the empty tomb, and He was present when the risen Jesus appeared to them in the upper room. But after receiving Jesus with heartfelt joy, something still weighed heavily on his heart. Peter now lacked confidence in himself. He believed in Jesus' resurrection, but did Jesus still believe in him?

Walking the Long Road to Galilee

After Jesus appeared to the disciples in Jerusalem, they learned He would meet them in Galilee (Matthew 28:7, 10). The journey to Galilee didn't just take a physical toll on their bodies. The long walk also gave the disciples time to reflect, not just on their journey, but on their moments of doubt and failure along the way. For Peter, each step may have brought back memories of the night he denied knowing Jesus. But it also stirred something more personal — a deep desire for his relationship with Jesus to be made right again.

Jesus had already given the disciples peace by breathing over them in Jerusalem. Yet Peter still longed to hear the words his heart needed most. He may have wondered, "Does Jesus still need me?"

A Private Conversation by the Sea

Jesus knew what weighed on Peter's heart and mind, so He pulled him aside. And not just for a casual conversation with a friend. Jesus was about to share a moment with Peter that was meant to heal something deep within his aching heart.

Three times Jesus asked Peter, "Do you love me?" And three times Peter answered, "Yes, Lord." Each time Peter responded, Jesus gave him a mission: "Feed my lambs. Take care of my sheep. Feed my sheep" (John 21:15–17). Jesus didn't just test or teach Peter; He restored him. He encouraged Peter to overcome what shame tried to take away — his true calling, which was to become the central leader of the early Church.

During their time together, Jesus did not talk down to Peter or scold him. Instead, He brought him even closer and entrusted him with the things that mattered most to Jesus. He knew Peter's greatest failure and doubts would shape his own faith, strengthen the other disciples, and lay the foundation of his future ministry.

From Restoration to Leadership

Sometime after meeting with Peter, Jesus also appeared to more than five hundred people at once (1 Corinthians 15:6). Peter might have been one of the many people who gathered to hear Him speak truth again, but this time as the risen Lord. As Peter listened, he stood there as a follower, as one who was forgiven and restored.

The guilt of denying the One he once followed no longer defined him. Peter was changing into the shepherd Jesus always knew he would become. The words Jesus spoke over Peter throughout His ministry were beginning to take root. Soon, Peter's voice would echo across the nations in Jesus' name, but only after his voice was renewed by the grace found in Him.

Yes, Jesus appeared to Peter to comfort him, but he also appeared to reawaken him. And with these simple words, "Follow me" (John 21:19), Peter discovered more strength and more purpose for the journey ahead than ever before.

Why This Story Matters

This story is a powerful reminder that even the greatest heroes in the Bible had imperfect pasts. Peter denied Jesus in His most painful moment, yet Jesus lovingly returned to restore him and send him forward. We are all called. We all have a purpose. And because of Jesus' death and resurrection, we don't have to stay chained to shame, sin, or regret.

Sometimes our past failures feel like labels we can't remove. Our minds are wonderfully made by the Creator, but they can also work against us when we allow fear and doubt to take control. We replay our mistakes and convince ourselves that we are no longer worthy or useful. Like Peter, we can carry shame for so long that it clouds our view of who we are in God's eyes.

But Jesus does not leave us in that darkness. When we surrender our doubt, depression, and brokenness to Him, He replaces them with healing, hope, and a renewed spirit.

With Jesus, restoration is always possible — our most broken moments can become the very foundation of our most meaningful calling.

A Prayer to End

Dear Jesus, thank You for seeing more in us than just our mistakes. When we feel unworthy or ashamed of our past, remind us that You didn't come to condemn us, but to restore us. Help us believe that Your grace is much larger than our largest mistakes, and that nothing we've done can separate us from You. Just as You did with Peter, encourage us, forgive us, and send us forward. May we walk humbly in Your forgiveness, ready to serve You with joy and confidence. Amen.

Bible References

Luke 22 — Peter denies Jesus three times
Matthew 28 — The disciples are told Jesus will meet them in Galilee
John 21 — Jesus restores Peter by the Sea of Galilee
1 Corinthians 15 — Jesus appears to more than five hundred people

The Great Commission — Carry the Message Forward

Back on the Mountain in Galilee

While in Galilee, the disciples reflected on their long and hope-filled journey since they first chose to follow Jesus. Each mile they walked with Him had been an opportunity to learn and grow, from hearing Him teach the crowds to watching Him transform lives, especially those on the fringes of society, the broken, the sick, and the poor.

Over the last few days, they pondered everything Jesus foretold, predictions that had now come true. Their resolve only deepened with each word they remembered. They were beginning to walk in faith again. Something was stirring inside them that they couldn't fully explain. They were no longer just followers; they were becoming leaders. But questions remained. What would Jesus say next? What would He ask of them? Where would He send them?

Jesus appeared once more when the disciples finally reached the mountain where He asked them to meet. Without words, He acknowledged each of them in a quiet yet powerful way. Some began to worship Him immediately, filled with wonder and joy. Others hesitated, uncertain about what they saw, unsure of what it all meant (Matthew 28:17). And yet, Jesus met each of them right where they were, some with bold faith and others who still wrestled with fear and doubt.

A Worldwide Mission

Jesus approached His disciples and spoke with a voice full of power and compassion. "All authority in heaven and on earth has been given to me" (Matthew 28:18). The One who now spoke in front of them no longer did so as a teacher, but as the Lord of all. He conquered death and ruled over all creation.

Then Jesus gave them the mission they were to carry forward that would define the rest of their lives and shape all mankind: "Go and make disciples of all nations, baptizing them in the name of the Father and of the Son and of the Holy Spirit, and teaching them to obey everything I have commanded you" (Matthew 28:19–20).

This wasn't just a checklist to get through in the moment. It was their mission, their lifelong purpose. Jesus entrusted them to carry the same message that had transformed their own hearts, the Good News of salvation. But He didn't ask them to share this message with those who lived near them. He wanted them to go out, near and far, to people from every nation, every language, and from every tribe across the world.

When the disciples heard Jesus' intent, some may have looked around and wondered how all of this could even be possible. They weren't trained teachers of the law; they were fishermen, tax collectors, ordinary men. But Jesus saw their potential. He saw what they could not see in themselves. He knew, with the power of His Spirit, they could become messengers of hope, carriers of truth, and builders of His Father's Kingdom, right here on earth.

A Promise to Go with Them

After charging His disciples with this work, Jesus assured them He wouldn't send them out alone. He gave them a promise that strengthened them then and still strengthens us today: "And surely I am with you always, to the very end of the age" (Matthew 28:20).

Jesus knew His disciples would face hard days, days when the mission felt too big and the opposition too strong. He understood that their path, like His, would be filled with danger. The religious leaders would continue to come after His followers in an attempt to silence the truth. But His presence would always be with them. No matter where their faith journey took them, through towns, deserts, palaces, or even prison, Jesus would remain by their side.

The time Jesus spent with His brothers on the mountain was more than a tearful goodbye. It was a moment of entrusting them with the work ahead. Jesus had done everything to prepare them for this calling. He had lived with them, taught them, fed them, and restored them. Now it was their turn to leave behind their old lives, go forward in the name of the Lord, and change the world.

Why This Story Matters

Jesus' command to "Go and make disciples of all nations," known as the Great Commission, wasn't meant just for the disciples who stood on the mountain that day; it is for everyone, including us. Jesus knew His disciples weren't perfect. Some were still unsure. But He gave them a life purpose anyway, and He promised to stay with them along the way.

This story reminds us that we are all invited to take part in a purpose far bigger than ourselves. We weren't saved so we could go back to our old lives with our old habits and selfish hearts. No, Jesus asks us to take what we have learned, what we have experienced, and tell others how His love has transformed our lives.

We may not travel to distant lands like His disciples, but we can share His Good News with those in our community. And we are never alone. His presence goes with us, giving us the words to speak, the courage to act, the direction to follow, and the perfect timing to fulfill the mission He has placed before us.

A Prayer to End

Dear Jesus, thank You for entrusting us to carry Your message forward. Help us remember we are each created intentionally, just as we are, to be used for Your good and perfect Kingdom. When we feel nervous or unsure, give us the confidence to live out our faith daily in all that we do. Teach us to stay faithful to the work You have given us, trusting that fruit comes in Your time, not ours. Amen.

Bible References

Matthew 28 — Jesus gives the Great Commission to His disciples

Jesus Ascends to Heaven

A Season of Hope and Wonder

The days after Jesus' resurrection were filled with wonder, healing, teaching, and power. The disciples witnessed the impossible in their leader and friend, Jesus, once crucified, now alive. He showed the disciples the wounds on His hands and side to convince them He was alive in the flesh and not a ghost. Plus, He ate broiled fish with them by the sea. But most importantly, as He walked and talked with them, He reassured them that He was truly risen (Luke 24:36–43; John 20:19–20, 27, 21:12–13).

For the next forty days after He rose from the tomb, Jesus appeared many times to His disciples and to other believers. He appeared to two men on the road to Emmaus (Luke 24:13–31). He appeared to Thomas and quieted his doubts (John 20:24–29). He appeared by the Sea of Galilee and restored Peter (John 21:15–19). And at one point, Jesus appeared to over five hundred people at once (1 Corinthians 15:6). His sightings weren't fleeting moments; Jesus spent time with His followers to teach, to expand their understanding of what was to come, and to help them see how everything written about Him in the law of Moses, the Prophets, and the Psalms had come true (Luke 24:44–45).

A Promise of Power

Jesus spoke and taught about the Kingdom of God and was very clear on this point: His followers were not meant to build this Kingdom on their own. He promised to send a Helper, the Holy Spirit. Jesus told them to stay in Jerusalem until the Spirit came upon them (Luke 24:49; Acts 1:4–5). This Advocate would strengthen them, not only for comfort and authority, but to confidently share His message everywhere, beginning in Jerusalem, then throughout Judea and Samaria, and finally to the farthest corners of the earth (Acts 1:8).

The disciples still had questions that were not yet answered. "Lord," they asked, "are you at this time going to restore the kingdom to Israel?" (Acts 1:6). The people had always imagined the Messiah would rise as a king and lead Israel back to power over its oppressors. But Jesus kindly reminded them that God's plans are revealed in God's timing. Their goal in the meantime? To be witnesses, to tell the whole world what they had seen and heard (Acts 1:7–8).

The Moment No One Expected

One warm afternoon, Jesus led His disciples out of the city, just beyond Jerusalem, to the Mount of Olives (Luke 24:50; Acts 1:12). This quiet hilltop was the backdrop of many moments in His ministry. Now, it would be remembered as the place of His departure.

Jesus lifted up His hands and blessed them (Luke 24:50). Then, right before their eyes, He was taken up. Slowly, gently, He rose into the sky until a cloud hid Him from their view (Acts 1:9). The disciples stood in awe, staring up toward heaven, their hearts pounding with wonder, trying to understand what had just happened.

While the disciples were still looking up, two men in white clothes appeared next to them. "Men of Galilee," they said, "why do you stand here looking into the sky? This same Jesus, who has been taken from you into heaven, will come back in the same way you have seen him go into heaven" (Acts 1:10–11).

A Joyful Return to the City

The disciples went back to Jerusalem filled with joy (Luke 24:52). Not sorrow, not doubt, but a deep and steady confidence. Jesus was no longer physically with them, that was true, but they were no longer afraid. They returned with clarity, confidence, and a renewed sense of purpose.

The waiting ahead was no longer uncertain. They were committed to their calling and ready to obey. The mission before them was clear: to share everything they had seen and heard, and to carry the message of Jesus to the world.

Why This Story Matters

Jesus did not leave His followers weary or confused. He filled them with confidence, instruction, and a powerful promise that would help them continue His ministry. His ascension was not the end of His story; it was the beginning of God's people being redeemed, set free from sin, and no longer separated from Him. It was a moment of transition as Jesus entrusted His disciples with the mission ahead, not with uncertainty, but with joy and encouragement.

Jesus' return to heaven also reminds us that His presence is still active among us. He reigns in heaven and on earth and will pray on our behalf when we call on His name. Every promise made by Jesus and the Father remains true, including the promise that one day, He will come again.

In this story, the disciples are told to wait for the Holy Spirit to come upon them. Jesus sent this Helper knowing they would need strength beyond their own. And how amazing it is that God knew we would need the same. Today, we do not have to wait. As followers of Jesus, we are given the gift of the Holy Spirit, the power and presence of God within us, to guide us, strengthen us, and reside with us all the days of our lives.

A Prayer to End

Dear Jesus, thank You for knowing we are incomplete without You. In Your great love, You sent us the Holy Spirit to guide us and give us confidence in who You created us to be. Help us learn to hear Your voice that dwells within us, so Your will may be done in our lives. Give us the courage to step into the mission You put before us. And help us live all of our days with joyful expectation, knowing that one day, You will return. Amen.

Bible References

Luke 24 — Jesus appears to His followers and ascends to heaven
John 20 — Jesus appears to His disciples after the resurrection
John 21 — Jesus restores Peter by the Sea of Galilee
Acts 1 — Jesus promises the Holy Spirit and ascends to heaven
1 Corinthians 15 — Jesus appears to more than five hundred people

Conclusion

As you finish this 47-day journey of walking beside Jesus, from His childhood in the Temple to His miracles, teachings, compassion, and ultimate sacrifice, I pray you have seen the depth of God's love for us. Every step, every story, every word that Jesus spoke pointed to a single purpose: to restore what was broken and bring us back into a close and eternal relationship with the Father.

Jesus willingly gave His life on the cross so our sins could be forgiven. He conquered death so we could live forever with Him. The Savior of the world did not stay in the tomb. He rose in victory, proving once and for all that nothing can stop God's love from reaching us.

But the story is not finished.

Before Jesus returned to heaven, He made a promise: that He would send the Holy Spirit, an Advocate, a Comforter, a Guide, to live within every believer. Through Him, we are never alone and never without the strength we need to live the life God has called us to.

This is where your story meets *His* story.

Now, I want to ask you the most important question anyone will ever ask:

Do you believe in Jesus?

Do you want to know Him personally, to surrender your life to Him, and to follow Him as your Lord and Savior?

If you feel God stirring in your heart, if you want to begin a new life with Him, or if you want to recommit your life to Him, you can pray these words:

A Prayer to Begin Again

"Lord Jesus, please forgive me of my sins and wash my heart clean.

I believe You are the Son of God and that You died for my sins.

I believe You rose again so I could have eternal life.

I give You my life. Help me follow You every day from this moment on.

Thank You for saving me and making me a child of God. Amen."

If you prayed that prayer today, heaven celebrates with you, and so do I. You are loved more than you know, and this is only the beginning of a beautiful journey with Jesus.

For all who have walked through this book, whether reading alone or as a family, I pray you continue to grow in faith and in the confidence that God's Spirit will guide you every step of the way.

Because the next chapter of God's story is full of power and purpose.

The Holy Spirit is coming.

In the final book of this trilogy, *The Thanksgiving Story: The Holy Spirit*, we will discover how God continues His work in and through His people, strengthening and equipping believers, uniting the followers of Christ, and empowering them to take the Good News to the ends of the earth.

Stay tuned.

The adventure is just getting started.

About the Author

Gabe Rodriguez is a husband, father, and business leader whose professional career has spanned sales, marketing, and strategic planning roles for some of the nation's leading retail and consumer product companies. Known for his creativity and ability to inspire teams, Gabe has spent years bringing innovative products to market and mentoring others toward growth and purpose.

After what he describes as years of lukewarm faith, Gabe experienced a spiritual awakening that reignited his heart for Christ and reshaped the direction of his life. That transformation led him to begin writing a devotional series centered on the Trinity, designed to help readers approach Scripture with confidence rather than fear, and to better understand the heart of God revealed through the Father, the Son, and the Holy Spirit.

Today, Gabe writes with the same passion that once fueled his professional career, but with an eternal focus: helping individuals and families build a faith that endures and is passed down from generation to generation.

Family Scroll

Now that you have completed this book, I encourage you to record your journey with *The Easter Story: The Son* in the Family Scroll. This is where you will document the first time, and every time after, that you have read or listened to Jesus' story of love, redemption, and restoration. Each entry is more than a note on a page. It is a marker in your walk of faith. Recording your understanding and belief in this story plants a seed of legacy, one that will grow long after you are gone. You can find more details on how to use the Family Scroll in the section at the front titled "How to Use This Book."

I was led to write this book as a real and practical way to pass my faith on to the next generation, and to offer a resource that would help others do the same. Part of the inspiration came as I read through Scripture, especially the first nine chapters of 1 Chronicles. These chapters are filled with names, generation after generation. At first glance, they may seem like simple lists, but they tell a deeper story — who God is, how He worked through families over time, and what legacy truly means. These genealogies helped each family know where they came from, which tribe they belonged to, how God fulfilled His promises, and why faith across generations matters.

The Family Scroll was born from that biblical example. In the following pages, you will find a sample to guide you, along with a blank Family Scroll for you, your family, and even your friends to begin recording your journey of faith year after year as you read *The Easter Story: The Son.*

A friend shared this quote with me:

"I have told you before that your mother and I will probably not be able to pass on to you any kind of earthly inheritance. If we can pass on to you a passion for God, however, we will have given you something more valuable than silver, gold, or rubies and more satisfying than anything a mortal can experience."

—John Piper, Don't Waste Your Life (Proverbs 3:13–15)

This is the heart of the Family Scroll — to pass on a faith that endures.

ℱamily 𝒮croll Examples

Example 1

- Gabe is married to Michelle, and they have two sons, Benjamin and Samuel.

- It is January 2018; Easter 2017 has passed.

- Gabe began reading or listening to *The Easter Story: The Son* in April 1998 and has recorded 20 years. Using one hash mark for each year.

- Michelle began in 2006 and has recorded 12 years.

- Benjamin began in 2014 and has recorded 4 years.

- Samuel began in 2016 and has recorded 2 years.

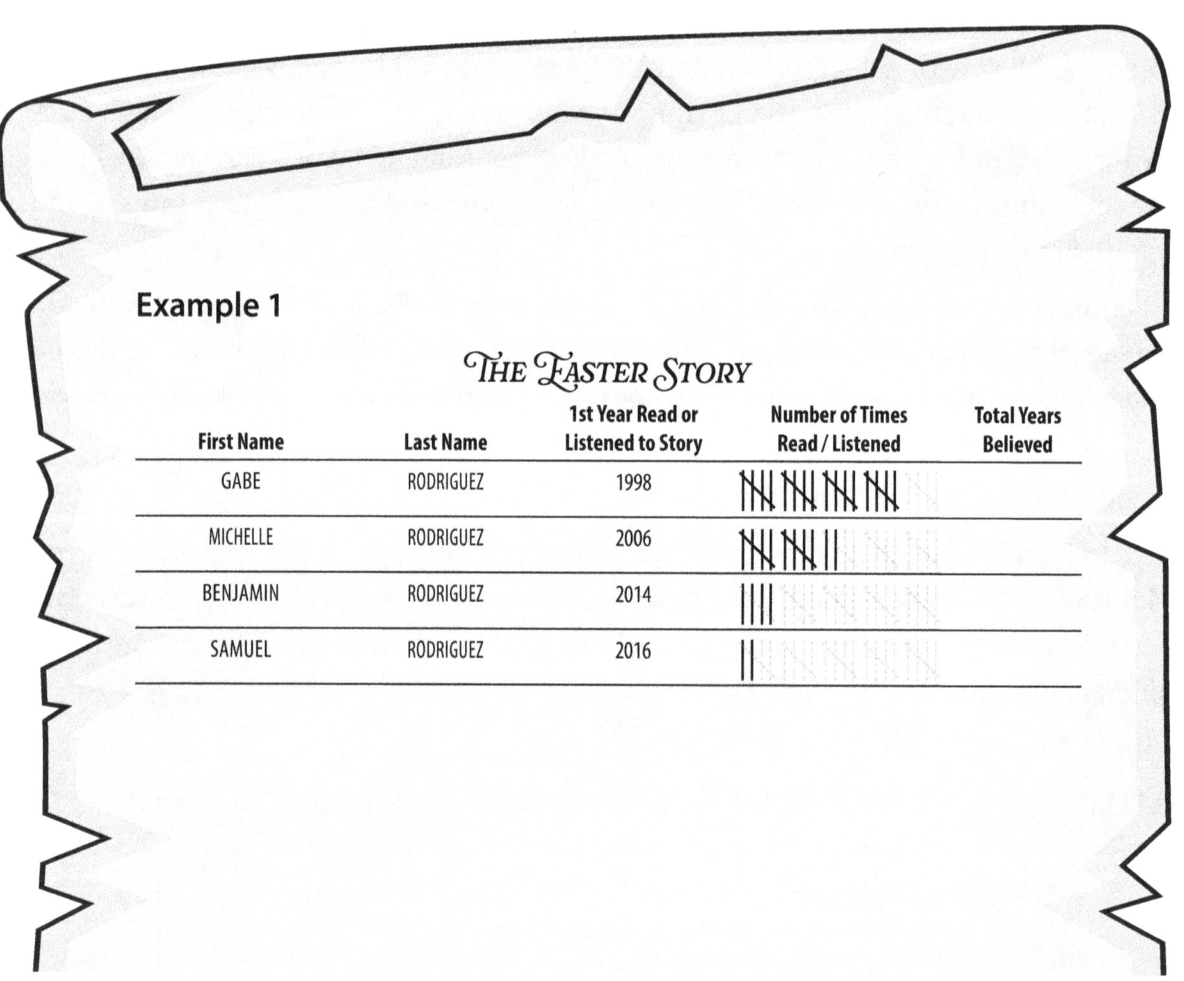

Example 1

𝒯he ℰaster 𝒮tory

First Name	Last Name	1st Year Read or Listened to Story	Number of Times Read / Listened	Total Years Believed
GABE	RODRIGUEZ	1998	|||| |||| |||| ||||	
MICHELLE	RODRIGUEZ	2006	|||| |||| ||	
BENJAMIN	RODRIGUEZ	2014	||||	
SAMUEL	RODRIGUEZ	2016	||	

Family Scroll Examples

Example 2

- Four more Easters have passed. It is now January 2022; Easter 2021 has passed.
- Gabe and his family have added 4 additional years to their Family Scroll, recording each year they have read or listened to the story.
- Benjamin is now a senior in high school.

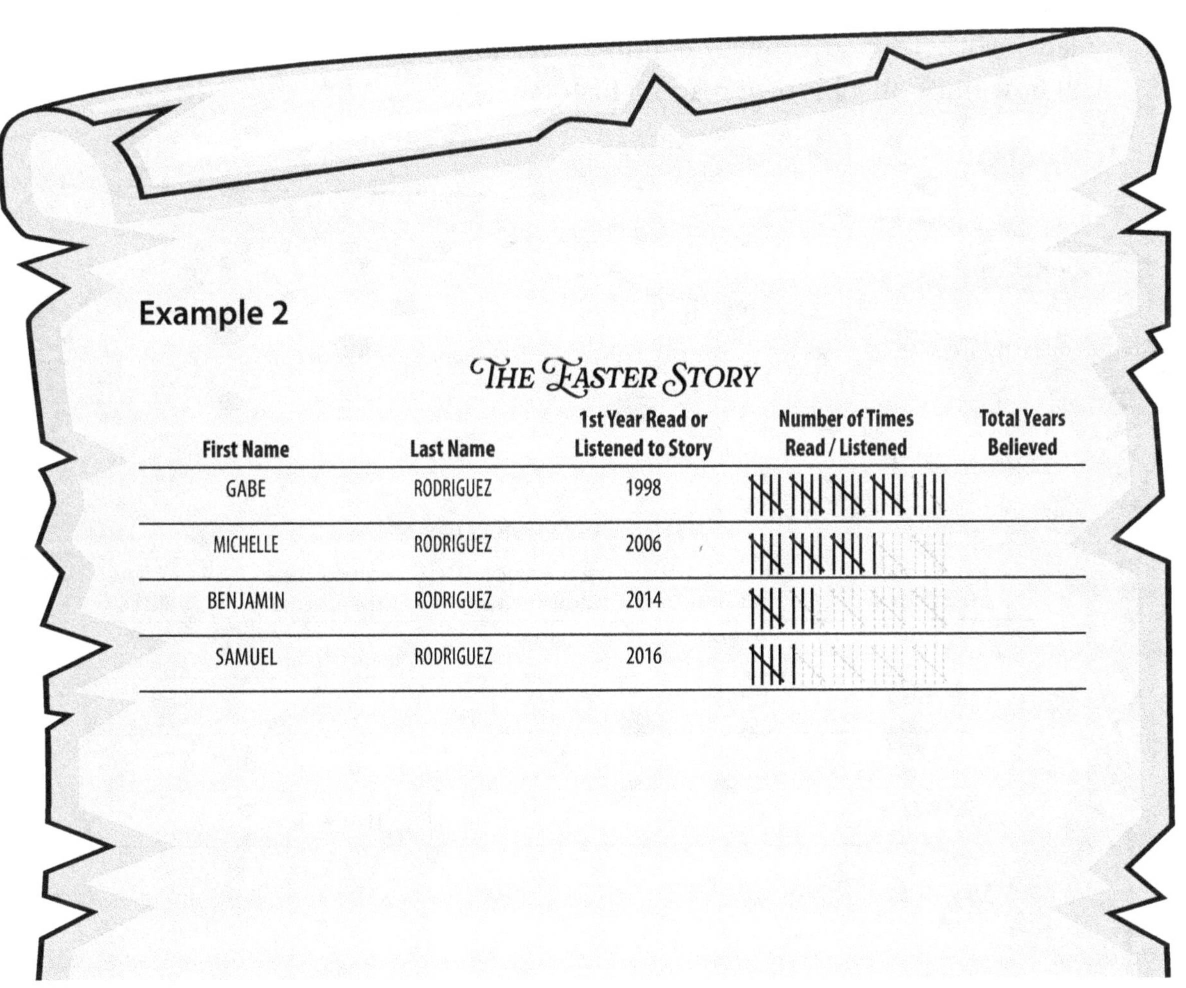

First Name	Last Name	1st Year Read or Listened to Story	Number of Times Read / Listened	Total Years Believed
GABE	RODRIGUEZ	1998	⦀⦀⦀⦀ (24)	
MICHELLE	RODRIGUEZ	2006	⦀⦀⦀ (16)	
BENJAMIN	RODRIGUEZ	2014	⦀ (8)	
SAMUEL	RODRIGUEZ	2016	(6)	

Family Scroll Examples

Example 3

- Benjamin is preparing to graduate from high school and leave for college; Easter 2022 is just around the corner.

- As an early graduation gift, his parents give him his own copy of *The Easter Story: The Son.*

- They transfer the number of years each family member has read, listened to, and believed the story using the Total Years Believed column.

- They also transfer Benjamin's running total using hash marks for each year he has participated in the tradition.

- However, they do not total Benjamin's years in the Total Years Believed column, because he is now continuing his own family legacy.

- From this point forward, Benjamin will no longer record the years his family (Gabe, Michelle, and Samuel) continues reading *The Easter Story: The Son*; he will now track only his own reading history.

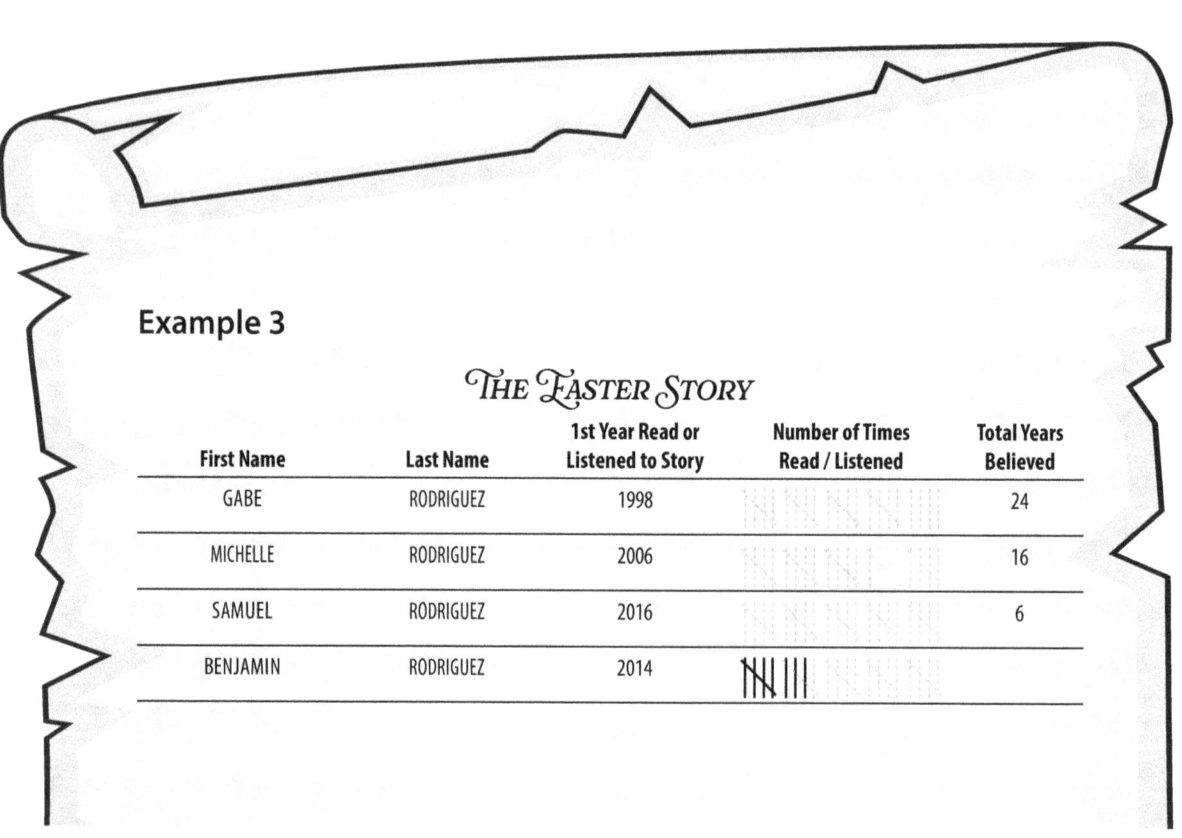

Example 3

THE EASTER STORY

First Name	Last Name	1st Year Read or Listened to Story	Number of Times Read / Listened	Total Years Believed
GABE	RODRIGUEZ	1998		24
MICHELLE	RODRIGUEZ	2006		16
SAMUEL	RODRIGUEZ	2016		6
BENJAMIN	RODRIGUEZ	2014		

Family Scroll Examples

Example 4

- The year is now January 2033. Benjamin has been in the workforce for 8 years.
- He married Rachel in March 2029, and she began reading or listening to the story that same year.
- When Benjamin and Rachel have children who are old enough to participate (not shown here), they will record their names in the Family Scroll, along with the year they first read or listened to the story, marking each year with a hash mark.
- The cycle will continue, just as it did in Example 3. When their first child leaves home, they will purchase a new copy of *The Easter Story: The Son* and transfer the family names and Total Years Believed into their child's Family Scroll.
- For example, if they have a son named Luke, the names transferred would include Gabe, Michelle, Samuel, Benjamin, and Rachel.
- The hope is that 40, 80, or even 120 years from now, each new reader in the same extended family will be able to see a lasting legacy of belief in the same story they now hold in their hands.
- And with that, the most important tradition continues — faith passed on from generation to generation.

Example 4

THE EASTER STORY

First Name	Last Name	1st Year Read or Listened to Story	Number of Times Read / Listened	Total Years Believed
GABE	RODRIGUEZ	1998		24
MICHELLE	RODRIGUEZ	2006		16
SAMUEL	RODRIGUEZ	2016		6
BENJAMIN	RODRIGUEZ	2014		
RACHEL	GARCIA	2029		

Family Scroll

The Easter Story

First Name	Last Name	1st Year Read or Listened to Story	Number of Times Read / Listened	Total Years Believed

Family Scroll

The Easter Story

First Name	Last Name	1st Year Read or Listened to Story	Number of Times Read / Listened	Total Years Believed

Family Scroll

The Easter Story

First Name	Last Name	1st Year Read or Listened to Story	Number of Times Read / Listened	Total Years Believed

Family Scroll

The Easter Story

First Name	Last Name	1st Year Read or Listened to Story	Number of Times Read / Listened	Total Years Believed

Family Scroll

The Easter Story

First Name	Last Name	1st Year Read or Listened to Story	Number of Times Read / Listened	Total Years Believed

Family Scroll

The Easter Story

First Name	Last Name	1st Year Read or Listened to Story	Number of Times Read / Listened	Total Years Believed